WHEN THEN IS NOW

Brendan Kennelly was born in 1936 in Ballylongford, Co. Kerry, and was Professor of Modern Literature at Trinity College, Dublin from 1973 until his retirement in 2005. He has published more than 30 books of poetry, including *Familiar Strangers: New & Selected Poems 1960-2004* (2004). He is best-known for two controversial poetry books, *Cromwell*, published in Ireland in 1983 and in Britain by Bloodaxe in 1987, and his epic poem *The Book of Judas* (1991), which topped the Irish bestsellers list: a shorter version was published by Bloodaxe in 2002 as *The Little Book of Judas*. His third epic, *Poetry My Arse* (1995), did much to outdo these in notoriety. All these remain available separately from Bloodaxe, along with his other recent titles, *Glimpses* (2001), a collection of short poems, and *Martial Art* (2003), versions of the Roman poet Martial.

His latest poetry book *Now* (2006) is published simultaneously with *When Then Is Now* (2006), a trilogy of his modern versions of three Greek tragedies (all previously published by Bloodaxe): Sophocles' *Antigone* and Euripides' *Medea* and *The Trojan Women*. His *Antigone* and *The Trojan Women* was both first performed at Peacock Theatre, Dublin, in 1986 and 1993 respectively; *Medea* premièred in the Dublin Theatre Festival in 1988, toured in England in 1989 and was broadcast by BBC Radio 3. His other plays include Lorca's *Blood Wedding* (Northern Stage, Newcastle & Bloodaxe, 1996).

His translations of Irish poetry are available in *Love of Ireland: Poems from the Irish* (Mercier Press, 1989). He has edited several anthologies, including *The Penguin Book of Irish Verse* (1970/1981), *Between Innocence and Peace: Favourite Poems of Ireland* (Mercier Press, 1993), *Ireland's Women: Writings Past and Present*, with Katie Donovan and A. Norman Jeffares (Gill & Macmillan, 1994), and *Dublines*, with Katie Donovan (Bloodaxe Books, 1995). He has also published two novels, *The Crooked Cross* (1963) and *The Florentines* (1967).

His *Journey into Joy: Selected Prose*, edited by Åke Persson, was published by Bloodaxe in 1994, along with *Dark Fathers into Light*, a critical anthology on his work edited by Richard Pine. John McDonagh's critical study *Brendan Kennelly: A Host of Ghosts* was published in The Liffey Press's Contemporary Irish Writers series in 2004.

His cassette recordings include *The Man Made of Rain* (Bloodaxe, 1998) and *The Poetry Quartets: 4*, shared with Paul Durcan, Michael Longley and Medbh McGuckian (The British Council / Bloodaxe Books, 1999).

BRENDAN KENNELLY

WHEN THEN IS NOW

THREE GREEK TRAGEDIES

BLOODAXE BOOKS

ISBN: 1 85224 743 6

First published 2006 by
Bloodaxe Books Ltd,
Highgreen,
Tarset,
Northumberland NE48 1RP.

www.bloodaxebooks.com
For further information about Bloodaxe titles
please visit our website or write to
the above address for a catalogue.

Bloodaxe Books Ltd acknowledges
the financial assistance of
Arts Council England, North East.

Cover design: Neil Astley & Pamela Robertson-Pearce.

Cover printing: J. Thomson Colour Printers Ltd, Glasgow.

Printed in Great Britain by
Bell & Bain Limited, Glasgow, Scotland.

CONTENTS

ACKNOWLEDGEMENTS

Brendan Kennelly's *Antigone* was first performed at the the Peacock Theatre, the Abbey Theatre, Dublin, on 28 April 1986. The text was first published in book form by Bloodaxe Books in 1996.

Medea was first performed by the Medea Theatre Company in the Dublin Theatre Festival at the Royal Dublin Society Concert Hall on 8 October 1988. It was revived on 6 July 1989 at the Gate Theatre, Dublin, prior to a tour of England which took in the Purcell Room at London's South Bank Centre. The text was first published in book form by Bloodaxe Books in 1991.

The Trojan Women was first performed at the the Peacock Theatre, the Abbey Theatre, Dublin, on 2 June 1993, with the text published by Bloodaxe Books launched at the first performance.

WHEN THEN IS NOW

Mythic drama is both immediate and distant. The immediacy enables a now-writer to stare into the past and invest it with the present and its problems. The distance enables that writer to stand back from, and at the same time confront whatever is troubling, hurting or inspiring him or her. Myth is both legendary history and acute prophecy, a fairylight that forms a bridge between realism and reality.

The term "myth" is frequently used nowadays in a pejorative or dismissive sense, whereas it was once used to convey a sense of power, passion, enduring significance: characters expressing themselves into a state of authentic being, mesmeric narrative, story begetting philosophical thought. The Greeks believed in belief; this is one reason for the terrifying freedom of their dramatic explorations. Almost every character in the best Greek plays seems to be on a passionate journey. That journey is also a journey through time, from *then* to *now*, but also, strangely and convincingly, from *now* back to *then*.

Time is a dance in which the dancers are constantly changing partners through whom they return to each other. The novelty of *now* always owes something to the accepted or rejected reality of *then*. It is a relationship not just between two points in time but also between two states of mind and/or body which always have the capacity to challenge and enlighten each other in ways not always acknowledged. Past, present and future are helpful labels but they can also be used as obstacles to our experience and understanding of a deeper fluency.

When Then Is Now brings together my contemporary versions of three Greek tragedies: Sophocles' *Antigone* (written around 440 BC) and Euripides' *Medea* (431 BC) and *The Trojan Women* (415 BC). All three plays dramatise timeless human dilemmas as relevant now as they were in ancient times. All focus on women whose lives are torn apart by war, family conflict and despotic regimes.

Writing these three plays helped me enormously at difficult times in my own life. *Antigone* came out of my heart and mind, following marriage break-up. Trying to understand Antigone herself was a special kind of education. This young woman, thousands of years old, made me reflect on courage and love. To this day, I admire the ways she spoke to me as I walked the streets of Dublin and Antwerp, grateful for her company, thinking of the lines she spoke through me. There's an element of healing present pain when one converses with the mythic world.

I wrote *Medea* in hospital, recovering from alcoholism. I actually began it in intensive care, having seen and heard a woman talking to herself aloud. She was addressing a cruel man who was coming up the road towards her house, and she knew that he would beat her up before the night was out. But she was beginning to protect herself: 'After you hit me, beat me in the kitchen and the bedroom, I'll lie there, and I know now that my moment of revenge is not far away. I'll be thinking of revenge when you're beating me tonight.' These words, or words like them, were in my mind and heart as I struggled with *Medea*. She must be one of the strongest and most terrifying women ever. She commits an unspeakably heinous crime, and then chariots into freedom, planning her life ahead.

Distance became immediacy when I embarked on *The Trojan Women*. The ancient city of Troy became a 20th-century Irish village, and Trojan citywomen became Irish villagewomen and, I believe, vice versa. Again, I think it was women's courage I was trying to explore and celebrate. I had seen it all around me as a child. I hope my version of *The Trojan Women* captures something of it.

These ancient plays are *then* illuminating *now*, like old teachers educating children who in turn will in some ways educate the un-born as they continue to learn from voices often forgotten but never completely lost, waiting always for, and willing to help, new, needy interpreters. Listening to ancient voices can help us confront, understand and express many problems of today.

BRENDAN KENNELLY
April 2006

SOPHOCLES'
ANTIGONE

A NEW VERSION

PREFACE

While writing *Antigone* I noticed that the characters seemed to come more and more alive with each re-writing as if, in this play where people are constantly judging others and being in turn constantly judged, they wish themselves and what they believe and do to be properly understood, to be accurately evaluated, to have justice done to them. Justice is of paramount importance in *Antigone*: and it is frequently in conflict with reality. I would define justice as a vision of what *should* prevail; reality I would define as the knowledge of what *does* prevail. Antigone is in the grip of her vision of justice and she wants to make it reality. Creon, too, is in the grip of his vision and he is determined to make it prevail. But Antigone's vision of justice, love and loyalty is not Creon's.

We have a conflict of visions, a conflict of two passionate people, two living hearts, brought about, perhaps ironically, by the dead Polyneices, or rather by attitudes among the living to the burial or non-burial of his corpse. Behind these conflicting attitudes are a number of histories: histories of family relationships, of personal values, of civil stability, of political change, of the growth of power and effective government, of ideas concerning what actually constitutes civilised living. These histories are like insistent, vigorous ghosts haunting every word that the characters say. This is a truly haunted play; the presence of the dead in the hearts and minds of the living is a fierce, driving and endlessly powerful force. This presence haunts the language and makes it, at certain moments, tremble with a peculiar intensity.

At the end, one is left with more questions than answers. What is the deepest source of Antigone's passion? What was Polyneices like? Why does Antigone feel with such unquestioning and unquestionable intensity about him? Are love and loyalty one and the same? What is Creon's concept of loyalty? What is Ismene's? What is Tiresias's? Haemon's? What is the influence of the dead on the living? I'm sure there are many people today who would reply – very little influence, very little indeed. But there are others who would reply in a very different vein. This version of *Antigone* tries to be true, to be loyal to my understanding of the Greek world; but it must also be loyal to my experience of life in Ireland, in the modern world. We are all both limited and stimulated by such experience. Family life. Brothers and sisters. Fathers and mothers. Moments of love and hate. Public life. Governments. Politicians. Rulers. People making speeches. People interested in power. People whose hearts and minds are moulded by power. People who betray, conspire and manipulate in order to achieve power.

So in any serious, sustained attempt to "translate" a play like *Antigone*, the conflict between past and present in the mind of the translator is as real as any conflict in the play itself. We are all, to some extent, creatures of conflict and, when we come to use words, we struggle to be true to our experience and understanding of that conflict. Conflict is served by the language it creates.

The ancient, original Greek infiltrates life in modern Ireland. In many ways, the past shapes and directs the present. The past educates and enlightens the present. The present selects from that education, that enlightenment, and makes its own way forward, as we all must, into a future that can be known only by experiencing it, and then only partially, depending on our willingness to give ourselves with whatever passion we are capable of into the arms of every moment that is waiting to be lived.

Antigone lives with passion because of her loyalty to, and love for the dead. But in living out her love for her dead brother she loses her love for Haemon, her living lover, Creon's son. There is a conflict between the claim of a dead brother and a living lover. This conflict is resolved 'in a black hole among the rocks'. Or is it? Will the consequences of what happens in that 'black hole' resonate among the unborn, the Antigones, Creons and Haemons of the future? The present is soon the past. The future becomes the present. The mills of consequence grind on.

Even now, after many re-writings, the more I think about this play the more questions present themselves. That fact is, perhaps, the truest testimony to the strange complexity and enduring attraction of *Antigone*.

BRENDAN KENNELLY
February 1996

ANTIGONE

Brendan Kennelly's *Antigone* was first performed at the the Peacock Theatre, the Abbey Theatre, Dublin, on 28 April 1986. The cast at the first performance was as follows:

ANTIGONE, *daughter of Oedipus*	Anne Byrne
ISMENE, *daughter of Oedipus*	Pauline McLynn
CHORUS	Peadar Lamb
CREON, *King of Thebes,*	
uncle to Antigone & Ismene	Kevin McHugh
FIRST GUARD, *a sentry*	Séan Campion
HAEMON, *son of Creon*	Darragh Kelly
TIRESIAS, *a seer*	Dónal Farmer
BOY	Seóna Ní Bhriain
SECOND GUARD, *a messenger*	John Olohan
EURYDICE, *Queen of Thebes*	Eileen Colgan
LADY, *attendant on Eurydice*	Maire Ó Neill
ELDERS & GUARDS	Donagh Deeney
	Micheál Ó Briain
	Macdara Ó Fátharta
	Condy Conarain
	Bill Cowley
DIRECTOR	Colm Ó Briain
SET AND COSTUME DESIGN	Bronwen Casson
LIGHTING DESIGN	Leslie Scott
MUSIC COMPOSED BY	Fergus Johnston
SOUND RECORDING	David Nolan
PRODUCTION MANAGER	John Costigan
STAGE DIRECTOR	Bill Hay
STAGE MANAGER	John Kells
ASM	Miriam Kelly
WARDROBE SUPERVISOR	Anne Cave
ASSISTANTS	Rita Sweeney
	Jane MacNally
MAKE-UP	Tony Delany
SET CONSTRUCTED BY	Peter Rose
DESIGN ASSISTANT	Geraldine O'Malley
PROPERTY MASTER	Stephen Molloy

ANTIGONE. (*To herself.*) Sickness. Creon. Law. My brothers. Dead.

> (*To* ISMENE.) Sister Ismene, do you know of any sickness,
> Of all the ills spawned by Oedipus,
> That Zeus does not curse us with?
> There's no shame, dishonour, ruin, pain
> Absent from your life and mine.
>
> And now, what do you make of this new edict
> Published by King Creon to all Thebes?
> What is the word? What have you heard?
> Or don't you understand that our friends
> Face the same doomed ends
> As our enemies
> In this city, and all through this land?

ISMENE. Antigone, not a single word of friends,
> Not a single happy or miserable word,
> Has reached me
> Since we two sisters
> Were robbed of our two brothers,
> Killed in a single day.
> Since the Argive host fled
> I might as well be dead
> Because I know nothing more,
> Not, as I have said, one solitary word.

ANTIGONE. I knew it perfectly well.
> That's why I brought you out here,
> Out of that court of sinister stone,
> Where you can hear the word
> All on your own.

ISMENE. What is the word?
> It's clear that you've been
> Brooding a long time on this.
> Antigone, even as a child,
> You were both broody and wild.
> What is the word, I say?

ANTIGONE. Creon has decreed
> That one of our brothers
> Should be buried with honour
> But that the body of the second
> Should be left unburied,

13

To rot in the heat of the sun,
Be eaten by birds,
Laughed at by men.
Children can throw sticks and stones
At our second brother's naked bones.
Our first brother, Eteocles, it is said,
With proper ritual and dignity
Is laid among the honourable dead.
But the corpse of Polyneices
Must remain unburied,
A thing of shame, unmourned,
A bit of trash
For claws to rip and tear
And beaks to feed on as they will.
Our dead brother's body, all rats and flies,
Must rot in the open air before men's and women's eyes.

That is the word, Ismene. Hear it well.
Brood on the word, dear sister. Action will follow.

Such is the word that Creon the Good
Has laid down for you and for me.
For me, do you realise, for me.
And he is coming here to proclaim the word
To all who do not know it.
Whoever disobeys the word of Creon
Will be stoned to death before the people.
Now that you know the word,
Now that my knowledge is yours, yours mine,
You will soon prove
The nature of your loyalty and love
And whether you are of noble blood
Or the slavish slut
Of a noble line.

ISMENE. If this is what Creon has said
    How can I disobey his word
    Concerning his treatment of the dead?

ANTIGONE. Brood on this: whether you
    Will join with me
    In doing what I have to do.

ISMENE. In what you *have* to do?
    What do you mean?

ANTIGONE. Will you help me
Bury Polyneices?

ISMENE. Would you bury him
When such a burial
Is forbidden by Creon,
Strongest of men?

ANTIGONE. Polyneices is my brother.
I can't be false to him.

ISMENE. But Creon's word forbids you.
Creon's word is law.

ANTIGONE. Polyneices is my brother.
Creon's word can never change that.
Creon has no right
To stop me doing what is right.
I will do what I believe is right.

ISMENE. Antigone, think how our father died
Amid scorn and hate,
His sins forcing him to blind himself
With his own hand:
Then his mother and his wife, the same woman,
One woman with two identities,
Hanged herself.
Finally, our two brothers,
In one day, forged their own doom,
Each killing the other.
And now, we two, mere women, are left alone.
Consider how we will die
If we disobey the word of Creon.
Remember this, Antigone:
You and I were born women.
We must not go against men.
I say
We are ruled by those who are stronger.
We must obey
Even when we do not believe
In our obedience.
We must obey in spite of disbelief.
That is my belief. Better to obey and live
Than disobey and die.
That is why I will obey Creon.

It is foolish to go against a strong man.
It is foolish to disobey his word.

ANTIGONE. Say what you say, be what you are,
      I will bury my brother.
      If I am stoned to death
      I will be with my brother.
      I have more love
      For the noble dead
      Than for the ambitious living.
      I would prefer to live
      Among the dead in love
      Than among the living in frustration.
      Ismene, live as you will.
      Dishonour, if you will, those laws
      Established in honour by the gods.

ISMENE. I do not dishonour the gods
      But I cannot defy the State.
      I'm not strong enough for that.
      A woman against the State
      Is a grain of sand against the sea.

ANTIGONE. I must bury my brother now.

ISMENE. I fear for you, Antigone. How I fear for you.

ANTIGONE. Don't fear for me. Fear your own fear.

ISMENE. At least, tell no one what you plan to do.
      Be secret. So will I.

ANTIGONE. Go shout it from the roof-tops, Ismene.
      Forget your despicable silence.
      Your silence will bring contempt on you
      In the end. Be true, not silent.
      Tell the blind, servile, murderous world
      What Antigone intends to do.
      If you're a coward, Ismene, at least be true
      To your cowardice. And don't try to turn me
      Into a secret version of your cowardly self.

ISMENE. You have a hot heart full of cold words.

ANTIGONE. I know what I have to do.

ISMENE. Do it if you can. But you would
    Try to do what no strong man
    Can do. If a man can't do it,
    How can a woman?

ANTIGONE. When my strength dies, that's when
    I cannot do
    What I must do.

ISMENE. But why attempt a hopeless task?

ANTIGONE. If that is your word, I will hate you
    And so will the dead.
    Leave me with my folly, Ismene.
    To suffer this is nothing
    To the suffering of a shameful death
    Or the pain of a cowardly silence.

ISMENE. Go, if you must,
    But of this be sure:
    Though your task is hopeless
    Those who love you
    Will always hold you dear.
    I love you, my sister.

Enter CHORUS.

CHORUS. The sun itself has saved our land
    Against the proud claims of Polyneices.
    He did his best and worst to destroy us
    But he was beaten back.
    Zeus always hates a boastful man
    And Polyneices was a braggart,
    A vain, arrogant, acquisitive braggart.
    Zeus cooled his proud tongue
    And brought him down to earth.
    A fallen braggart is a sad sight,
    A laughing-stock in the mocking light.

    Zeus saved us from the braggart's tongue and arm,
    From his desire to bring our people harm.
    Zeus brought the braggart low.
    Zeus flipped the coin of battle
    And gave us victory.

And now that we have victory,
Bring on infinite wine.
We'll drink and dance and sing the dark away
Until we stand triumphant in the applauding light of day.

The word is victory for superior men
Who do what they must
While Polyneices corrupts in dust.

But look, here comes Creon, our king,
Our new king because of new fortune
From the gods. Creon is fresh and new
And wise too.
Why has he summoned the wise old men?
What word has he for them?
What word has he for the people?
For all of us who have ears to listen?
What is the word of Creon?

Enter CREON.

CREON. Friends, the State is stable once again
        After being threatened by a treacherous man.
        I have called you here because I know
        How loyal you are to this city, this State.
        It is your loyalty that makes us great.
        When Oedipus ruled this land, and when he died,
        Your loyalty never weakened for a moment.
        You are loyal to what is right.
        Yours is the proper kind of pride.
        Since then, the sons of Oedipus,
        The sons of his wife-mother,
        The sons of two women in one,
        Have killed each other.

        Now, I occupy the throne.
        My friends, I have come into my own
        Because I am close to the dead
        And understand the laws they gave to living men.

        No man can be known in spirit, mind and soul
        Until he understands law and rule.
        That is my word to you.
        If any leader of the State,
        Through fear, keeps his best counsel secret,
        I count him a base man.

18

And if any puts a friend above his country
I count him a man of treachery.
I would not be silent if I saw
My people threatened.
Who can be silent on such matters
If he is loyal to his people?
Who can be silent if he understands the law?
It is the law that keeps our country safe
And if our country's safe, why then we will be friends.
Law is a worker. It works for justice.
Law enables justice to happen as it should, as it must.

That is the rule that will protect this city.
Following that rule, I give you my edict
Concerning the sons of Oedipus:
Eteocles, who died fighting for our city,
Will be buried in full dignity
And rest among the noble dead.
Polyneices, his brother, who came back from exile
And tried to destroy by fire
The city of his fathers
And the shrines of his fathers' gods,
To murder his own brother
And lead our people into slavery,
Polyneices will not be buried.
His corpse will never rest
In the private dignity of the earth.
His corpse must corrupt in the open air,
His corruption must be seen by all, witnessed by all,
Dogs and birds will eat his flesh and bones,
Children throw stones at him for sport,
Shouting his name in mockery,
'Polyneices! Polyneices!
Man of shame! Corpse of shame!'
That will be his special fame.
That is my word.
The wicked are not the just
And must not be treated as if they were.
We have a city to maintain.
It will be maintained by rule, by law,
By men who understand that truth.
These are the men I will honour
In life and in death. My heart is loyal
To loyal hearts.

CHORUS. That is your word, Creon,
　　Regarding this city's enemies and friends.
　　You have the power to turn your word to action
　　For the benefit of all of us,
　　Both living and dead.

CREON. Make sure, then, that you guard my word.

CHORUS. Let that be a job for some younger man.

CREON. No, watchers of the corpse have been discovered.

CHORUS. What then do you require?

CREON. That you never take the side of those
　　Who break my word.

CHORUS. If a man did that, he'd simply be
　　Bringing about his own death.

CREON. That is true; but men have often betrayed
　　The truth for money. You are loyal.
　　Make sure you never sell your loyalty for money.

Enter GUARD.

GUARD. I give you my word on this –
　　I didn't know whether to come quickly or slowly.
　　I said to myself 'You eejit, you're
　　Going to your doom.'
　　And I said to myself 'What, you old slowcoach!
　　If Creon hears this from someone else's lips,
　　You'll die for it.'
　　And so I argued with myself,
　　Making a short road long, making that long road
　　A road of doubt and pain.
　　At last, however, I decided I should come here
　　And tell you every word. I would be open and plain.
　　The worst that can happen to me is my fate.
　　No man can sidestep that.

CREON. What's wrong with you?

GUARD. I want you to hear my own word first:
　　I did not do the deed
　　Nor did I see who did it
　　And yet I want to tell you
　　So that no harm will come to me.

20

CREON. You're a shrewd man
    And know how to protect yourself.
    You obviously have strange words to say,
    Strange news to tell.

GUARD. I have. But bad news is hard to tell.

CREON. Come on, man, out with it.

GUARD. Someone has buried
    The corpse of Polyneices.
    Someone sprinkled dust on the flesh
    And observed the rites that piety demands.
    Whoever did this
    Went away unseen, unheard.
    I give you my word.

CREON. What are you talking about?
    What man alive would dare to do this thing?

GUARD. I don't know.
    There was no sign of spade, shovel or pickaxe.
    The ground was like a rock, unbroken,
    And not a trace of wheels.
    Whoever did it left no hint or sign
    And when the morning-watchman showed it to us,
    A kind of troubled wonder filled us all,
    The wonder at one with the trouble.
    We couldn't see the dead man;
    He wasn't shut in a tomb
    But lightly covered with dust
    As by the hand of someone
    Who wished to shun a curse.
    And there was no sign
    That dog or bird or beast
    Had torn the corpse.

    Then we, the guards, accused each other
    In foul and vicious language.
    We might even have killed each other.
    We were ready to walk through fire,
    To swear to the gods
    That we had nothing to do with it.

    At last, one guard said
    The whole thing must be reported to you.

Not one word must be kept secret –
The whole thing must be told to you.
Only a bad guard would be silent on such a matter.
We drew lots to see who should bring the news.
So here I am, chosen to tell you the story;
I am unwelcome, I am unwilling,
No man wants to the be bearer of bad news.
I bring the truth.

CHORUS. O King, I have been thinking:
Might not this be the work of the gods?

CREON. Quit that foolish talk
Before you drive me mad with rage.
When you say the gods care for this corpse
Your words are foolish, blasphemous, insane.
Why should the gods hide the nakedness of one
Who came to burn their treasures and their shrines,
To flatten their city and destroy its laws?
Why should the gods honour the wicked,
Do homage to the treacherous?
No, not the gods, never the gods!
    From the beginning
There were certain people in this city
Who resented my words
And spoke against me,
Muttering in secret.
They were not content to obey
Like all the people happy with my rule of law.

It is they
Who have bribed others
To commit this crime, this blasphemy.
They have spent money on this crime.
Money is the greatest evil men have known.
Money destroys cities
Maddens men from their homes
Twists decent souls till they
Will do any shameful thing.
Of all evils, money is the King.
It offends the gods
Because money is godlessness.
And it makes a slave,
A dangerous slave, of the man who gives his mind to it.

Whoever did this deed for money
Will pay the price.
And now, I give you my word on this:
If you don't find the man who buried Polyneices
And bring him here before my eyes,
You will be strung up alive
Before you die.
Why?
That you may learn
Not to take money from any source,
Not to sell your soul for money
Not to set your heart on money
Not to blind your eyes with money
Not to spend your days thinking and dreaming of money.
You will find that money
Brings you ruin, not prosperity.

GUARD. May I speak a word? Or should I just leave?

CREON. Even now your words offend me.

GUARD. Are your ears offended, or your soul?

CREON. How would you know where and how I am offended?

GUARD. The deed offends your mind,
My words offend your ears.

CREON. You're just another prattler of this city.

GUARD. Perhaps. But I did not cover
Polyneices with dust.
I am loyal to you. I bring the truth.

CREON. More likely you sold your soul for money.

GUARD. I find it sad
That one who should be a fair-minded judge
Should so misjudge me.

CREON. To hell with all this talk
Of judge and judgment.
If you don't bring to me
Whoever did this deed
You'll find that money
Is the truest source of sorrow.

GUARD. Well, may the culprit be found
And brought before you for judgment.
But one thing's sure –
I'm not so eager to come here again.
For this,
I owe the gods great thanks.
Telling the truth is a dangerous business.

Exeunt.

CHORUS. Wonders are many
And none is more wonderful than man.
He possesses the power that outstrips the sea
Driven by the storm-wind
Beating the waves that threaten to engulf him.
He has the power of Earth,
Eldest of the gods,
Eternal, untiring,
Turning the clay with horses and ploughs
From year to year to year.

Man, genius, wit, prophet, poet,
Thinker, worker, sage,
Controls the hearts of birds in flight,
The hearts of prowling beasts,
Beasts roaming the hills.
He tames the wildest creature,
Makes him accustomed to the yoke.
Man is strong and wise and beautiful.

He tames the mountain bull.

He tames the wild life of words
The mad life of thought
All the dangerous moods
Of heart and mind.
He copes with frost and hail and rain.
He does not flinch from pain.
Only death defeats him,
Death, master of the master.

Baffling even to his own mind
Is the skill
Which brings him now to evil,
Now to good.

When he honours the laws of the land
When he upholds the justice loved by the gods,
Secure and proud is his city.
Whoever dishonours the laws of the land,
Scorns the justice loved by the gods,
That man has no city, no right to live in a city,
That man must live where no one lives.
Never may he visit my home,
Never share my thoughts.
That man must know his madness is his own
And is not part of the people, not part of the city.
He is a severed limb,
A severed head, a mad outcast,
Unacceptable to the loyal living
And the restful dead.

Enter GUARD, *leading* ANTIGONE.

What's this?
My soul is stunned.
Antigone?

O luckless daughter of a luckless father –
Oedipus!
What does it mean?
Antigone – a prisoner?
Antigone – breaker of Creon's laws?
Antigone – captured in an act of folly?

GUARD. Here's the girl who did it.
We caught her in the act of burying the corpse.
Where is Creon?

CHORUS. Look, he's coming from the house.
He's needed now.

Enter CREON.

CREON. What's happening here?

GUARD. My King, a man should pledge his word
Against nothing, for later action will belie that word.
Today, I gave my word to myself
I'd never set eyes on you again
Because my soul winced under the lash of your tongue.
But now I have come, bringing this girl
Who was captured as she buried Polyneices.

25

Here she is. Take her. Question her.
Grill her as you will. But now
I am free, finally, of this trouble.
I told you I am loyal to you.

CREON. This girl – how was she captured?

GUARD. Burying the corpse.

CREON. Do you know what your words mean?

GUARD. I saw her burying the corpse. Your words
Decreed the corpse should not be buried.
Are my words clear? I saw this girl
Burying her brother's corpse.

CREON. Yes, but how was she seen?
How was she captured?
How did all this happen?
Tell me how it happened?

GUARD. When we reached the place where the corpse was,
I could feel the threat of your curses above my head
Beating like the wings of maddened birds
About to swoop and rip my brains and heart out.
I brushed away the dust covering the corpse
And showed again its naked corruption.
Then, with the other guards, I sat down
On the hillside, to windward, in case
I'd be cursed by the stink of that corruption.
Every guard, alert, kept the next man alert
With a fierce stream of threats and curses.
Curses kept us all awake and watchful.

We sat there till the sun began to burn.
Suddenly, a whirlwind wrenched from the land
A storm of dust, blind confusion in the sky,
Darkening the plain, befouling every tree and flower.
I could hear the heavens choking, strangled by the dust.
I closed my eyes, and bore this curse of the gods.

How long that dust raged in its own madness
I'll never know. But when it calmed and dropped,
I saw this girl. She gave a sharp cry
Like a wounded bird or a mother
Brutally stripped of her children.

26

When she saw the corpse deprived
Of the covering dignity of dust,
She cried a cry beyond all bounds of words
And cursed whoever did that deed.
Immediately, she went and got more dust
And once again, began to cover the dead.

At this point, we rushed forward,
Took her. She offered no resistance.
We accused her of what we'd seen.
She denied nothing, to my joy, to my pain.
To my joy, because I'd escaped your curses.
To my pain, because I had to bring this girl
To judgment. Something about her is so
Noble, so unafraid.

Yet, to be honest, what matters most to me
Is that I'm safe now.
Safe, although I told the truth.

CREON. You, girl, staring at the earth,
Do you admit, or do you deny,
This deed?

ANTIGONE. (*Looking up.*) I admit it, man.

CREON. (*To* GUARD.) Go. You are free.

GUARD *leaves.*

CREON. (*To* ANTIGONE.)
Did you know my edict had forbidden this?

ANTIGONE. I knew it. It was public knowledge.

CREON. But yet you dared to break the law?

ANTIGONE. Yes. Yours is the word of a man,
Not of a god. I had to bury my brother.
I know I must die; that is a grief.
But to have left a dead brother unburied
Would have grieved me infinitely more.
If I seem foolish to you, this may be
Because you are a foolish man, a foolish judge,
Spreading your word with foolish law.

CHORUS. This is the daughter of Oedipus.
She bows before nobody and nothing.
Her heart is fire. Her mind is ice.

CREON. Yet, there are times when the proudest spirits
    Are most likely to be humbled.
    I've seen the wildest horses tamed by a little curb.
    This girl offers a double insult:
    First, she broke the law;
    Second, now, she boasts of that breaking
    And delights in what she has done.
    A mere girl offers a King a double-insult.
    How will a King endure it?
    How will any man endure it?

    I would be no man,
    She would be the man
    If I let her go unpunished.
    Although she is my sister's child
    She must be punished.
    And so must her sister.
    I charge *her* with conspiracy in this
    Burial of a brother.
    Summon the sister.
    I saw her in the house just now
    Muttering to herself.
    Guilty people mutter much.

ANTIGONE. Would you do more than kill me?

CREON. No.

ANTIGONE. Why do you delay, then?
    Your words repel me.
    My words must be the same to you.
    I sought to bury my brother.
    That is my word, my deed.
    Word and deed are one in me.
    That is my glory.
    And that is what the people think
    And would say
    If they were not afraid of you
    Who have the power
    To say what words you will,
    Do what deeds you will,
    And call it law. Law!

CREON. With these words, you differ
    From all the other people of this city.

ANTIGONE. No, my words are theirs, theirs mine,
But they seal their lips for fear of you
And the high-and-mighty horror of your law.

CREON. Are you not ashamed to act
Differently
From all these other people?

ANTIGONE. No. It is no shame to love a brother.
It is my love that makes me different.
It is my difference that you fear.

CREON. Your second brother – did he not die
For another cause?

ANTIGONE. Brother by the same mother and the same father.

CREON. Why then do you do something hateful,
Odious, damnable in that other brother's eyes?

ANTIGONE. He's dead and honourably buried.
How can you know
What his words might be
If he stood here before you now?
Do you presume to know the mind of the dead?

CREON. Would you make the honourable brother
Equal with the wicked?

ANTIGONE. It was the honourable brother's brother that died –
Not his slave. His brother, do you understand?
A brother is a brother anywhere, any time,
On earth, in heaven, or in hell.

CREON. Yes, but one brother fell
Attacking the law, the city, the land.
The other died defending them.

ANTIGONE. Nevertheless, I desire that burial.
So do the gods.

CREON. In law, which is our sanity and hope,
The good cannot be treated like the bad.

ANTIGONE. What's evil on this earth,
May seem blameless in the gods' eyes.
You may be the King of fools, Creon,
Though you believe you're wise.

CREON. We must live on this earth.

ANTIGONE. Yet never forget the possible difference
　　Of that other world of the gods.
　　Thinking of difference there
　　May make us different here.
　　Creon, you fear the thought of difference.

CREON. An enemy is not a friend,
　　Not even in death, or beyond.

ANTIGONE. I have no wish to school myself in hate.
　　I want to love.

CREON. Go, then, to your dead, and their difference.
　　If you want to love,
　　Love your different dead.
　　For you, girl, the dead are most real.
　　While I live, no woman
　　Will tell me how to think and feel;
　　Above all, how to rule. I know how to rule.
　　That's why I know I am not a fool.

ISMENE *is led in.*

CHORUS. Look, here comes Ismene, crying,
　　Like the loving sister she is.

CREON. You're no woman, you're a snake
　　Slithering through my house
　　Waiting to sting me with your poison.
　　How could I know
　　That I was nourishing two snakes
　　To poison me from my throne
　　And make me the sad corpse of a King?
　　Now, do you admit
　　Your part in this burial?

ISMENE. Yes, I admit my part.

ANTIGONE. No, that is not true.
　　You did not agree to the deed.
　　You had no part in it
　　Nor did I allow you any part in it.

ISMENE. You are in trouble now, my sister.
　　I want to be at your side.

ANTIGONE. The gods and the dead
    Know it is I
    Who covered the corpse of my brother
    With dust.
    Your words must not belie that fact.
    A sister in mere words
    Is not a sister that I love.

ISMENE. Dearest sister, do not turn me away,
    Nor turn away your head.
    Let me die with you
    And so honour the dead.

ANTIGONE. You will not share my death
    Nor claim to have done something
    Which you have not done.
    My death will do.

ISMENE. My life is nothing without you.

ANTIGONE. Ask Creon; you've got
    Such respect for him.
    You always thought a lot of him.
    You are loyal to his law.

ISMENE. Why do you hurt me, noble blood,
    When it does neither of us any good?

ANTIGONE. If I mock you now, Ismene,
    I mock you out of deepest pain.

ISMENE. Say whatever words you will.
    Let me serve you now with body and soul.

ANTIGONE. You'll serve me best by saving yourself.

ISMENE. Have I, then, no share in your fate,
    Your death.

ANTIGONE. You chose to live for fear.
    I chose to die for love.

ISMENE. At least I made a protest at your choice.

ANTIGONE. There were two worlds, two ways.
    One world approved your way,
    The other, mine.
    You were wise in your way,
    I in mine.

ISMENE. Yet we are both accused
  Of the same offence.

ANTIGONE. You will live, my sister, and follow
  Your days and nights to their proper end.
  My life is an act of service to the dead.

CREON. Look, one of these girls has just shown
  How foolish she is. The other
  Has been foolish since her days began.

ISMENE. That's how it is, O King.
  Nature gives us reason
  But there are moments when we squander
  Our dearest gifts.

CREON. You squandered the sweet gift of reason
  When you chose to die with her.

ISMENE. What is my life without her life?

CREON. Do not speak of her 'life'. That girl is dead.

ISMENE. But will you kill the girl
  Who is to marry your own son?

CREON. There are other fish in the sea
  Other roads to travel
  Other fields to plough.
  Antigone was a living woman once. She's dead now.

ISMENE. But never again can there be such love
  As bound these two together.
  Their two hearts are one.
  If Antigone dies, so does your son.

CREON. My son cannot marry one
  Who has committed such a crime.
  How can an unrepentant, arrogant, blasphemous criminal
  Marry my son?

ANTIGONE. Haemon, Haemon, my beloved.
  Your father wrongs you deeply now.

CREON. No more words out of you!
  No more words about marriage
  To my son!

CHORUS. Will you deprive your own son of this girl?

CREON. Death is her husband now.

CHORUS. Creon is determined Antigone must die.

CREON. Yes, I am determined.
      Determined for you, for me,
      Determined for the laws of this land,
      This city,
      Determined for the Kings
      Who will succeed me,
      Determined for today, tomorrow,
      The living, the unborn.
      You know me now. I am determined Creon.
      (*To the* ATTENDANTS.) Take these
      Inside. From now on, treat them
      As women – keep your eye on them.
      Don't give them too much scope.
      Even the boldest woman tries to escape
      When she looks death in the face.
      So hurry, servants, hurry! Take them away!

CHORUS. Blessed are they whose days are free of evil.
      When a house has been cursed by heaven
      It rages from age to age of its people.
      Not a single soul can be forgiven.

      Sorrows of the dead are heaped on sorrows of the living,
      Sorrows of the living heaped on sorrows of the dead.
      Generation cannot be freed by generation
      But each is undeliverable, stricken by some god.

      There is a power no human power can touch,
      There is a law no human law can understand,
      Through the future, as through the past, this law holds good,
      No great force enters mortal life without a curse.

      What comforts some men is deceit to others
      And neither knows if what he feels is true:
      Brothers will love sisters; sisters, brothers,
      And when that love is spent, what will they do?

      A man will think until his mind is fire
      Till good is evil, and evil shines like good;
      A mischievous god may play with his desire
      But who knows how to play with a mischievous god?

33

Look, Creon,
Here comes Haemon,
The last of your sons.
Is he grieving for the doom
Of his promised bride, Antigone?
How bitter is his heart
For the thwarted hope of his love
Or rather
For his marriage sentenced to death
By his father? Do you dare
Sentence your son's future to death?
Do you dare call yourself his father?

Enter HAEMON.

CREON. We'll soon know the answers to your questions.
      Haemon, my son, do you come in rage
      Against your father, now that you know
      Your bride-to-be is put to death by him?
      Or do I have your filial good-will
      Whatever I may do? Are you loyal to me,
      Loyal and true?

HAEMON. Father, I am your son, and will obey
      Whatever the words of your great wisdom say.
      What marriage could be a greater gain
      Than a father's wise guidance for his son?

CREON. Law governs all happiness,
      And this should be your heart's fixed law –
      Obey your father's will in everything.
      Fathers toil painfully towards their wisdom
      But joyfully give that wisdom to their sons.
      This is a father's dearest dream –
      To see dutiful children grow around him in his home,
      To see his children hate his enemies
      And love his friends, just as he does himself.
      But the man who fathers undutiful children
      Makes trouble for himself
      And triumph for his enemies.
      To ward off chaos, a family must still
      Be moulded by the father's will.
      A father
      Is the maker of the future.

And so, my son, do not surrender
Reason to pleasure.
Reason is a king,
Pleasure, a perfumed slut of one night.
Pleasure is sweet weakness,
Reason, stern might.
Pleasure soon grows cold in sweating arms,
You find a treacherous woman shares your bed.
The more treacherous she is, the sweeter are her words.
There's nothing as sweet as treachery.
Now, one true word I have to tell –
This girl will find her true husband in hell.
She has admitted open disobedience.
She sneers at me. No King's voice can still her
Voice. I will not betray my people.
I will kill her.

Let her appeal till she is dead
To the fact that we are kindred.
Disobedience is the worst of evils –
It destroys cities
Maddens men from their homes
Twists decent souls till they
Will do any shameful thing.
Of all evils, disobedience is the King.
It offends the gods
Because disobedience is godlessness.
Obedience is the key to fairer living.
Therefore, we must not allow
A disobedient woman
To tear us apart.
If I must fall from power
Let it be by a man's hand,
Never by a woman's.

CHORUS. Creon, your words seem wise.

HAEMON. Father, the gods have given us the sweet gift of reason,
The most humane and priceless of all their gifts to men.
I lack the skill to say where your words are wrong
And yet another man may have a helpful thought.
For your sake, I listen to what all men say,
Your dreaded frown does not encourage people to be
Truthful. But I have heard them muttering in dark places

Concerning this girl, such words
As would offend your ear:
    'Why should such a girl,
Who did such a noble thing,
Meet such a shameful death?
When her brother died in battle
She would not let him be unburied
To be devoured by beasts and birds and dogs
But shrouded him in the dignity of dust.
Far from deserving death,
Does not this girl
Deserve every golden honour
The State can offer?'

Such are the words that circulate in secret.
Father, nothing matters to me like your welfare.
I want you always to prosper.
Do not persist, then, in one mood alone.
The world is full of different words, different voices.
Listen to the words, the voices.
Do not be a prisoner in yourself
Although you are a King of others.
For if any man thinks that he alone is wise,
Then, my father, he's in danger of being mad.

I beg you, permit yourself to change,
Do not embrace the madness of being fixed
Forever in yourself. If you love your people,
You will listen to them. If you listen
To your subjects, you will be a greater King.
The only object of a great King
Is to be greater still.
So listen well.

CHORUS. Father, listen to your son.
    Son, listen to your father.
    Learn from each other.

CREON. Is a man of my age and experience
    To learn from a boy of his limited sense?

HAEMON. I say nothing that is not right
    Insofar as I understand what is right.
    If I am young, consider my sense,
    Not my years.

CREON. How can I honour disobedience?

HAEMON. I do not wish you to show respect
For anyone who does wrong.

CREON. (*Furious.*) She has done wrong.
She knows she has done wrong.

HAEMON. (*Calmly.*) The people say that she has done no wrong.

CREON. Shall the people tell me how to rule?

HAEMON. Listen to the people, for now you speak
Like an inexperienced boy.

CREON. This is my land. This land I have to rule.
Must I listen to the voice of every fool?

HAEMON. No man can rule alone.
No single city belongs to any single man.

CREON. Is not the city the creation
Of the ruler's vision?

HAEMON. You'd make a good King of the desert.
The sand would never disagree with you.
Neither would the rats.

CREON. You speak for women.
You speak for this girl.

HAEMON. If you are a woman
My love is for you.
I work for your good fortune.
That is my word, father. My word is true.

CREON. Are you mocking me?
Are you openly defying me?

Haemon. No, I tell you you do not listen.
Why do you not listen to me?
Why do you not listen to your people?
What else is justice
But listening to the voices of the people
And then, with the help of the gods,
Deciding what is right?
Father, you offend justice.

CREON. How do I offend justice
When I respect my own judgment?

37

HAEMON. You do not respect justice
When you trample on the voices of the people.

CREON. You do not mean the people.
You mean woman.
You would put a man below a woman.

HAEMON. Insofar as I understand
What is happening here,
I try to be fair.

CREON. You are pleading for that girl.

HAEMON. I plead for her
For you
For me
And for the gods above and below,
The gods who whisper in my heart.

CREON. You will never marry her now.

HAEMON. Then she must die, and by her death
Destroy another.

CREON. You dare to threaten me?

HAEMON. What threat is there
In fighting such stupidity?

CREON. You'll regret this.

HAEMON. You'll regret your speaking of regret.

CREON. You sad little boy, you woman's slave,
Out of my way.
Go, be a woman
Since you understand the thing so well,
Be a woman like the woman
Whose brother was condemned to rot in public hell.

HAEMON. You would speak
But not let me speak?

CREON. Now, by the gods, hear my word.
You shall suffer for making me
Suffer your mocking disobedience.
Bring forth that girl,
That hated thing, to die
Here, now, before his eyes,
The criminal bride at the mocking bridegroom's side.

HAEMON. No, never at my side shall Antigone die.
    Never again shall you look upon my face.
    Rave and rage as best you can
    Among the friends who still consider you a man.
    You have your loyal friends, my father.
    They tell you all the lies you want to hear.

Exit.

CHORUS. Your son is gone.
    The man is gone, O King,
    In angry haste.
    A pure and youthful mind, when hurt,
    Can lay the world to waste.

CREON. He is no man. My son is not a man.
    So let him do or dream what he can.
    He'll not save these two girls
    From their doom.

CHORUS. Are you going to kill them both?

CREON. No. Thank you for that just thought.
    I wish to be just, I wish to be fair.
    I will not kill that girl
    Whose hands are pure.
    Thank you for that question.
    Your question has saved her life.

CHORUS. And how will you kill Antigone?

CREON. I will take her to the loneliest place in the world.
    It is a hole among the rocks,
    A black pit of emptiness.
    I will give her food,
    But she must live forever
    In that dark hole, blacker than any midnight.
    There, let her do as she will –
    Pray to the gods, they may rescue her
    If they are able.
    I want Antigone to think of her life
    As she lies in that black hole
    Among the rocks,
    Why she broke my law,
    Why she did not believe each word
    That in all sincerity I said;

Why, above all, she mocks the lawful living
And gives her love
To the shameful dead.
I want Antigone to think,
To think until she knows
In every corner of her being
Why she wasted her life
For nothing.

Exit.

CHORUS. Love, you are the object of our lives,
    Love, you are the truest crime;
    Love, you prove the obscenity of money,
    Love, you are a waste of time.

    Love, you live in the heart of a girl,
    Love, you are the spittle on an old man's lips,
    Love, you are a suburban nightmare,
    The soiled lace-curtains from which a heart escapes.

    Love, you help a child to grow up,
    Love, you fill the eyes of a young bride;
    Whatever they say of you, O love,
    You're always dying, yet never completely dead.

ANTIGONE *is led out to her execution.*

    Now, I move beyond the bounds of loyalty,
    All Kings I scorn, for Antigone I cry,
    Antigone, passing to the darkness
    Where she must die, Antigone
    Whose fiery heart would never let her tell a lie.

ANTIGONE. I go on my last journey,
    Looking my last on the sunlight.
    Because I have given my life to the dead
    I have never stretched in the marriage-bed.
    I'll never know the thrust of living blood,
    The Lord of the Dark Lake I shall wed.

CHORUS. You go to the dead,
    Without plague or sickness on your head.
    You have chosen and shaped your own fate
    Unlike these women
    Who have to prowl among men

Or other women
For their little pleasures.
You have created your own solitude.

ANTIGONE. I am afraid of my fate,
As if it were something
That might choke me
Like a chicken-bone
Stuck in my throat.
Why do I think of eternity
As choking me
Like ivy choking a house?
My hands leap to cover my eyes.

CHORUS. Your hands at your eyes!
So it was with many a goddess.
And, like many a goddess,
You must keep your hands before your eyes.

ANTIGONE. Mock me, if you will.
I do not doubt that you are able.
You are used to flattering men.
But I am a woman
And must go my way alone.
You know all about men,
You know all about power,
You know all about money.

But you know nothing of women.

What man
Knows anything of woman?

If he did
He would change from being a man
As men recognise a man.

If I lived,
I could change all the men of the world.

I go to live in a hole in the rocks.
Think of me there.

I am a woman without fear
In a hole in the rocks
Where no man or woman dare venture.

CHORUS. You have gone to the utmost edge of daring
 And you have fallen.

 Is this because of your father's sin,
 Old horny Oedipus? He knew two women in one.
 Is this his legacy to you? A hole in the rocks. Black hole.
 Alone.

ANTIGONE. You have touched my deepest fear.
 You have opened my father's head.
 You have looked into my mother's bed.
 You know why I have given my life
 To the unburied dead.

 And now I go to them.

 I go to my father, foolish boy,
   foolish lover, foolish man.

 I go to my mother, kind soul,
   foolish woman.

 I go to my brother whose corpse
   I sprinkled with dust.

 I go to the gods, the gods' beds,
   the gods' lust.

 O my loving brother, my love for you
 Has robbed me of my life.

CHORUS. Antigone, you have destroyed yourself.

ANTIGONE. I go alone.
 Let no one weep for me.
 Let no friend think of me.
 I never knew a man
 Or heard his worlds upon a wedding-night.
 I walk a cold road to my death.
 It's no use now
 Looking back
 Or looking forward.
 I go alone.

Enter CREON.

CREON. Take her away!
> When you have placed her
> In that black hole among the rocks,
> Leave her there, alone.
> Banished from the world of men,
> This girl will never see the light again.

ANTIGONE. That black hole among the rocks
> Will be my prison
> Bridal-chamber
> Tomb.
> From there I go to my father,
> My mother and my brother.
> My brother! It is for you I suffer this.
> This is my reward for loving you.
> And yet I only gave you what was rightly yours.
> If I had been the mother of children,
> If I had a husband in my home,
> I would not have done for them
> What I did for you.
> Why do I speak such words?
> A lost child can be replaced
> And other husbands can be found.
> But when my father and mother are dead
> No brother's life
> Can ever flower in me again.
> In me flourished the very best of men.
> Men!
> Creon!
> He sends me to my grave
> Because I acted out my love.
> I never knew the marriage-bed
> I heard no bridal song
> I knew no happy married love
> No joy of children.
>
> What law have I broken?
> My crime was love.
> Loving my brother was my sin.
> That is the law of man.

CHORUS. The girl is torn in all directions!

CREON. Let these damned guards be quick.
> Take her away.

ANTIGONE. These words are stones
Battering me to death.

CREON. You have no hope, girl.
You are going to die.

ANTIGONE. Men are leading me to death.
Men made the law that said I'm guilty.
Men will place me
In a black hole among the rocks.
Men will deny me light.
Yet all I did was for a man
Whom other men called evil.
Because I would not kill my love,
My love kills me.
In this place, killers of love go free.

ANTIGONE *is led away.*

CHORUS. Imagine! A daughter stuck in a black hole,
Buried alive in a hideous pit
Among the rocks!

A daughter!

She is the light of life
The better part of a man's blood
The transformation of crude manhood
Into a creature to be loved by men
She is the reason for his being
She opens him up to himself
Through her he may know himself
And know more deeply the proud pain of love

A black hole among the rocks
No light
No light

Buried alive

Victim of love
Victim of law

Daughter in the darkness

Blind to the world of men

Enter TIRESIAS, *led by a boy.*

44

TIRESIAS. Creon, it takes a boy
    To lead an old blind man
    Into your presence.

CREON. Tiresias, what brings you here?

TIRESIAS. Listen to my words.

CREON. I have listened to them before.

TIRESIAS. Yes; and when you listened,
    Things worked well for you
    And for your city.

CREON. That is true.

TIRESIAS. Listen, Creon. There is a knife at your throat.

CREON. What – what do you mean?

TIRESIAS. I sat in the light, listening
    To the wings of birds.
    The birds were mad with rage.
    As they ripped each other in the air
    I listened to the voices of their wings.
    I heard what the voices said.

    In fear, I offered sacrifice
    But I could make no fire.
    Instead, the flesh oozed from the bones.

    The bones were naked in the sun.

    I asked this boy to tell me what was wrong.
    I listened to the boy. The boy had listened to men and women.
    I know now that you have poisoned this city
    By refusing burial to the corpse of Polyneices.
    The gods refuse all sacrifice and prayer
    And the birds of the air are mad
    Because they have eaten the flesh
    And tasted the blood
    Of the rotting corpse
    Of the son of Oedipus.

    Listen to me, Creon.
    Think of my words, and act on them.
    Bury that corpse.

CREON. You are an old man.
You see things.
We agree you are a seer.
Seeing is your trade.
For all your seeing in the past, you were well paid.
Take money where you will
But do not tell me
What to do with that corpse
Just because someone has given you money.

TIRESIAS. Who knows what – ?

CREON. What are you saying?

TIRESIAS. Who knows what truth is in the words of those
Who come to you, offering
The wisdom of their hearts and minds?
Are you prepared to listen to good words?

CREON. Yes, but not to foolish talk.

TIRESIAS. You are foolish, Creon.

CREON. I'll let that insult pass.
I'll not insult you, Tiresias.

TIRESIAS. You *do* insult me, when you say
My words are foolish.

CREON. Seers and prophets
Always had a weakness for money.

TIRESIAS. And the children of tyrants
Always corrupted the State.

CREON. Do you know, old man,
You are speaking to your King?

TIRESIAS. I know it well: for by my words
You saved this city.

CREON. I approve your wisdom
But not your love of evil men,
Not your love of the corpse.

TIRESIAS. Would you make me speak the words
That create dread in my soul?

CREON. Speak your words – but not for money.

TIRESIAS. No hope of that from you.

CREON. Speak!

TIRESIAS. One of your own blood will be a corpse soon
  Because you have condemned to darkness
  A daughter of light
  And because you have left unburied
  One who belongs to the gods.
  You have violated a law
  And continue to do so.
  That is why you will be punished.

  In a short time
  There will be wailing in your house.
  All the cities of this land
  Throb with hatred for you
  Because dog and bird and beast
  Carry the pollution of the unburied corpse
  Through all their streets
  Until it fills their houses
  Reeks at their tables
  Infects their children
  And poisons the very bed of love.

  You asked for my words.
  You have them now
  And every word is true.
  Creon, the birds of the air have told me
  That you spread evil everywhere.

  Boy, lead me to my home
  And let this ignorant King
  Meddle with younger men.
  Let him learn to keep
  A temperate tongue in his head.
  Let him learn respect
  For the living and the dead.
  Let him think
  All day, all night
  Until he begins to suspect
  He may not be always right.

Exeunt.

CHORUS. Tiresias has spoken cutting words
    And his voice is always true.

CREON. His words trouble my soul.
    But how can I give in now?
    Yet not to surrender
    May bring destruction.

CHORUS. Listen to my words.

CREON. Speak.

CHORUS. Release the girl.
    Bury the corpse.

CREON. Is this your word to me –
    That I surrender?

CHORUS. Yes, and quickly too.

CREON. Quickly? This is monstrous.
    And yet if I – if I do not –
    Yes, yes, I must obey.
    I must change my mind.

CHORUS. Free the girl yourself.
    Bury the corpse yourself.
    Do not wait for others.

CREON. Yes, I'll go as I am.
    I'll free the girl
    And bury her brother's corpse.
    But why now, even now, do I break
    My own law? Why do I break the law
    That all my life I worked and struggled to uphold
    For the good of my people? My own people?

CHORUS. A change of mind, a change of heart
    Allows the gods to play their part.
    If the change take place in a stubborn King
    Is there hope of further blessing
    Breathing from the stars' deep fires
    New words to rectify old mad desires?
    Is the change of heart in time?
    Or too late?
    Whose in the law? Whose is the crime?

I send my words like birds into the sky
Turning to black dust in a cloud of anarchy,
Nightmare of law, perfect folly of human art,
You see and witness all, god of the change of heart.

We fix and label you with whatever names we will
You smile at every name's bewildering syllables,
The ease with which the dead rip the living apart,
Bread upon your table, god of the change of heart.

Fixed mountain, restless river suggest the family is good,
Law and ritual would cage the demons in the blood,
What must a King do, if his son is a rebel upstart?
Your lightest mood may shock the land, god of the change
    of heart.

To persist in one conviction is to set teeth against a stone,
To believe in one thing only is to live with a word alone,
A man burns others with his words, choosing his special mark;
Pity that triumphant man, god of the change of heart.

Your toy is time, your child is man, he plays on the world's
    floor,
Loving, judging, cursing, erring – but always wanting more;
And more he gets, and more he gets, while you sit still, apart;
Turn horror to delight
Suffering to song
Misery to joy
Hatred to love
Curses to blessings

But will the mind see in time

God of the change of heart?

*Ente*r MESSENGER.

MESSENGER. Creon saved our land
        And was once a blessed man.
        Justice sweetened his every word.
        Then he changed
        And became like a living corpse,
        All the joy
        Drained from his soul.
        And now he must face new grief.

CHORUS. What grief?

MESSENGER. His son is dead. Haemon is dead.

CHORUS. How?

MESSENGER. By his own hand,
    In hate and rage at his father.

CHORUS. Tiresias, your words are true!
    Here is Creon's wife, Eurydice.

Enter EURYDICE *and her* ATTENDANT.

ATTENDANT. My Lady, why are you so distressed?
    You should have returned to rest
    In your own house.
    As you were passing through the gate
    You stopped, as if stricken,
    And muttered something about words
    That knew no mercy.
    Wherever they came from,
    Whatever they said,
    They stole the wholesome colour from your face
    And turned your living beauty
    Into the very picture of death.
    And yet, it is not too late for you to rest.
    Your mind will find sweet peace again
    Because your heart is blessed.
    Let these merciless words
    Fly out of your heart like lunatic birds
    Into the indifferent skies,
    Rip each other to pieces
    Where no human eyes
    Can see their madness rage
    In wing and beak and claw,
    No human ears
    Hear their lost, last cries.
    Dear lady, speak to me
    As you have spoken to me all these years.
    What words did you hear?
    Why did you grow pale and tremble
    As though with some unbearable fear?
    Why did your body shake in terror
    When your hand rested on your own familiar gate?

Look at me, dear lady, I am here
As I have always been here.
Here.
Why do you stare
As though the only purpose of your life
Is to make a clear word
Doubly clear?

EURYDICE. (*Staring at her* MESSENGER.)
I heard these words as I was going to pray.
My heart became a place of prayer,
Happy to speak out of its own silence
To the listening silence of my god.
But the words that shaped my prayer
Were strangled by your words of murder.

(*She moves towards the* MESSENGER.)

Murder! Do you hear me? Murder,
Although you did not use that word.
I heard everything you said
But my heart, my mind, my blood
Will not believe my son is dead.
Dead! How can my son be dead?
You speak as if from another country,
A land of more-than-human grief.
Between us
Is a sea of disbelief.
I am drowning in that sea.
No prayer that I have said,
Or hoped to say, or dreamed but left unsaid,
Can lighten my heart now.
Death and disbelief are the air I breathe today,
This killing air, merciless and raw.
And yet I know I must believe
What is.
Not to believe what is
Would bring worse pain
If such can be imagined.
Your words of cruel truth are now my only law.
Your words! I will hear your words again.
Come near! Come near! Tell me what you saw.

MESSENGER. Dear lady, I will tell you what I saw.
    I went with Creon to where the corpse lay.
    We washed it
    And raised a mound of his native earth.
    We turned, then, to free the girl
    From that black hole in the rocks.
    I heard this crying from that place
    And hurried with Creon there.

        As the King approached,
    He seemed clothed in those cries.
    He groaned in pain and said
    'I hear my son.' Again: 'I hear my son.'

        I went in among the rocks.
    I saw Antigone hanging by the neck.
    I saw Haemon
    With his hands around her waist,
    Crying of his lost love
    And in the same breath
    Cursing his father.
    The words of love mixed fearfully with the words of cursing
    In that hole among the rocks.

    Creon begged his son
    To come into the light
    But the boy glared at him
    With maddened eyes
    And tried to kill his father
    With his great cross-hilted sword.
    He missed his aim.
    And then he leaned his body on the sword
    And drove it through himself.
    With his last breath
    He embraced Antigone.
    Then it was corpse embracing corpse
    In the black hole of death.

Exit EURYDICE.

CHORUS. Why has Eurydice left without a word?

MESSENGER. I don't know. Perhaps to grieve in private.
    I'll go into the house and find out.

Exit.

52

Enter CREON *with* ATTENDANTS *bearing the body of* HAEMON.

CREON. My son, dead by his own hand,
But more by stubborn and killing words:
My son.

CHORUS. Is the change of heart in time?
Too late. Witness the crime.

CREON. What made me so cruel?
What made my heart
So stubborn and hard?
Why was I so cruel and blind,
An upright corpse of cruelty?

Enter MESSENGER.

MESSENGER. Your queen is dead.

CREON. Mercy!
Is there no mercy in the world?
I am a dead man.
Eurydice, my dear, dear wife –
Dead. All dead.

MESSENGER. She stabbed herself
And died heaping curses on your head.

CREON. Is there anyone to kill me?

MESSENGER. With her dying breath
Eurydice blamed you
For the deaths of Haemon and Antigone.

CREON. Eurydice – she killed herself?

MESSENGER. Yes, as I have said.

CREON. Your word is wrong.
I killed Eurydice.
Whatever future waits me now
Is only days and nights of guilt.
I live to pollute the world.
Let me die, please, please, let me die.

CHORUS. There is a future,
You must cope with that.
There is a present,
We all must cope with that.

There are so many things to do
In this land, this city.

CREON. Not long ago, that thought
Was a good dream filling all my life.

CHORUS. Dream no more.
Live with what you are.

CREON. What am I?
A foolish man –
I killed my son
I killed my son's love
I killed my wife
I killed my happy self.
Wherever I look now
I see accusing ghosts,
I hear only
The accusing words of the dead.
Why did I not listen to the words of the living?
Why did I not listen?

Exit.

CHORUS. To be wise is to be almost happy.
The god's laws
Are the laws we must observe.
Our little strength is nothing
Set against their might
And the ringing words of proud men
Are children's frightened whispers in the night.

ANTIGONE

Endnotes by
TERENCE BROWN
KATHLEEN McCRACKEN

TERENCE BROWN

An Uncompromising Female Spirit

Oedipus King of Thebes is dead. His two sons Eteocles and Poly-
neices have fought a fratricidal war for the succession which has
left them both dead too. Creon is now king and has issued an
order that whereas Eteocles can be buried with all appropriate ob-
sequies, Polyneices' corpse must be left to rot – prey to bird, beast
and dog. The protector of the city will be honoured, the rebellious
exile must suffer opprobrium even in death: 'The wicked are not
the just/And must not be treated as if they are'. Oedipus's daugh-
ter Antigone will have none of such politic judgement. The ancient
pieties must be observed, even on pain of death. So she acts. Per-
forms ritual service for her kin. So tragic devastation is wrought
upon a doomed household.

This starkly simple plot which the Western imagination has in-
herited from fifth-century Athens (the plot may indeed originate
with Sophocles' text) has had a recurrent life in the very many
versions of it which poet and dramatist have attempted in modern
times. It has been in periods of particular civil and political strife
that it has most profoundly appealed. The early 19th century for
example, in the wake of the French Revolution and the Napoleonic
imperium, canonised Antigone as sacrificial victim, proto-Christ. Her
death spoke of the crushing of aspirations to sexual and personal
liberation that the revolution had unleashed. And it was during the
Nazi occupation of Paris that one of this century's most resonantly
political Antigones came to life in Anouilh's version.

The conflict which this play dramatises, between *real-politik* and
unyielding principle, between the social requirement that order be
maintained and the absolute demands of ancestral piety is a con-
flict made painfully real in many of the crises that have challenged
this nation in the recent past. That such conflict is symbolised in
a battle of wills between a powerful man and a vulnerable but in-
domitable young woman must have peculiar significance for a soc-
iety undergoing a protracted and often fraught adjustment of its
fundamental attitudes to sexuality. It touches some of our deepest
anxieties, echoes our intimated hopes.

Brendan Kennelly's version of the *Antigone* is absorbed by two
things: the mysterious gulf between words and deeds and the claus-
trophobic intimacy of family life. The first of these finds expression

in the work's admiration for an Antigone for whom word and deed are one. The second is expressed in the play's stark highlighting of the terms of familial and sexual relationship – brother, sister, child, father, daughter, husband, wife, boy, son, girl, woman, man. It is as 'man' that Antigone chooses to address King Creon at her moment of pure rebellion. An uncompromising female spirit declares itself in radical opposition to Creon's male authority.

A poet's fascination with a figure in whom word and deed are one is what links the author of this version to those 19th century romantics who found in Antigone a symbol of a total integrity of being, who saw in her a sacrificial victim, a scapegoat. That Brendan Kennelly also re-creates the legendary plot as a family romance, as a domestic tragedy whose victim is Creon as well as Antigone tells us that the 20th century must experience this Sophoclean drama in the light of lessons derived from another of the master's works, the tragedy of King Oedipus.

April 1986
Reprinted from the Peacock Theatre programme for *Antigone*.

KATHLEEN McCRACKEN
Site of Recovery: Brendan Kennelly's *Antigone*

Brendan Kennelly has written versions of four classic plays: Sophocles' *Antigone*, Euripides' *Medea* and *The Trojan Women*, and Lorca's *Blood Wedding*. All four allow for the extension of themes and techniques present in his earlier writing and pose challenges which are valuable to Kennelly both in his development as a writer and in terms of the issues he would put to a contemporary Irish audience. Indeed, he follows an established practice among modern and contemporary Irish poets. From Yeats's *King Oedipus* and *Oedipus at Colonus* and MacNeice's *Agamemnon* through to the spate of recent versions (including Tom Paulin's *The Riot Act* and *Seize the Fire*, Aidan Carl Mathews' *Antigone*, Seamus Heaney's *The Cure at Troy*, Desmond Egan's *Medea* and Derek Mahon's *The Bacchae*), the technical challenge of translating, adapting or, as has more often been the case, transposing or interpreting classical Greek dramatic texts has been bound up with the impulse not just to create 'parables for our times' but also with a need to re-examine precisely those binary oppositions and 'specific universals' which George Steiner, in his seminal study of the Antigone myth, identifies: 'the confrontation of justice and law, of the aura of the dead and the claims of the living...the hungry dreams of the young [and] the "realism" of the ageing'.[1]

Although a comprehensive study of the connections between these Irish versions has yet to be made, Anthony Roche's essay 'Ireland's *Antigones*: Tragedy North and South'[2] gives a detailed analysis of four versions of *Antigone* scripted in 1984: Paulin's *The Riot Act*, Mathews' *Antigone*, Kennelly's *Antigone* and Pat Murphy's film *Anne Devlin*. Roche finds Kennelly's version 'the least obviously Hibernicised' in terms of idiom and political metaphor, and certainly if we were to place Kennelly's versions alongside those of his contemporaries his would appear comparatively apolitical. If Kennelly's version of *Antigone* is less overtly political, if it is more conservative in its interpretation of the original text, this is in part because his interest lies not so much in Paulin's parabolising of certain figures and events in Irish and Northern Irish politics, or in Mathews' experimentation with postmodernist stagecraft (though both tactics are to some degree implicit in his project) as in stressing the feminist imperatives and, by extension, the broad humanist ramifications, which emerge naturally out of Sophocles' play. Roche proffers an astute feminist reading of the play, and, of the three male-authored versions he considers, concludes that Kennelly's pushes furthest in this direction, but that it too falls short of being a 'truly feminist Antigone'. 'Having brought us to the edge, Kennelly can go no further, both because his literary source does not and because that "black hole" is a woman-centred space towards which none of the three male writers…can do more than gesture'.[3] Since *Antigone*, Kennelly has gone well beyond this point. In the three plays which have followed he has moved progressively further into that 'woman-centred space' which, almost a decade ago, may well have seemed off-limits. Consequently we are able to reconsider Kennelly's *Antigone* both in its own right and as the foundation for his move into drama.

The signal issue debated in Kennelly's *Antigone* is well-defined by one of his literary touchstones, Blake's dictum 'True progress is possible only between opposites'.[4] Kennelly's belief that Ireland's difficulties are rooted in the failure of 'closed minds' to embrace that which is other and opposite, whether in terms of historical reality, political and religious affiliation, gender or nationality, is concretised in the clash between the play's protagonists, Antigone and Creon. Indeed, the multitude of versions of *Antigone* produced from the sixteenth through to the present century, its fascination over and above virtually any other Greek tragedy for writers as diverse as Hegel and Hölderlin, Freud and Jung, Brecht and Anouilh, can be attributed largely to the fundamental dualities embodied in the play's characters. The problem, and the tragic source, in *Antigone* (as in each of the plays Kennelly has adapted) is that these opposites, however much they may reflect one another, remain irreconcilable.

Steiner contends that the excellence of Sophocles' play resides in its expression of the five major conflicts which govern the human condition. These he conveniently lists as: 'the confrontation of men and of women; of age and of youth; of society and of the individual; of the living and of the dead; of men and of god(s)', and goes on to analyse how, in their initial encounter, Antigone and Creon epitomise each category.[5] In opting to emphasise the dialectic of genders in his version, Kennelly has also chosen to highlight the drama's fundamental opposition. In doing so he is not, needless to say, breaking new ground. The subject of the play lends itself to a feminist interpretation, so it is not surprising that a number of feminist versions had appeared prior to 1984. But as Steiner is careful to note, it was not until the 1960s and the advent of 'women's liberation' that Antigone's radical feminism is championed over Ismene's generic conservatism. The prototype for subsequent stage productions in this vein was New York's Living Theatre interpretation for German audiences of Brecht's version of Hölderlin's translation, which instructs that 'Only women's authentic liberation, only the utter refusal of Ismene's *notre sexe imbécile*, will break the infernal circle...the false coupling of men and women in a traditional social order'.[6]

Kennelly adopts a comparable position in that, in his version of *Antigone*, the drama becomes a site of recovery where women are afforded expression of their 'unrestricted humanity', the male/female confrontation is centralised, and female rights, whether to despair, to connive, or to rage, are exposed as elemental to both the impact of the performance and to human nature. In constructing his play Kennelly was working out a clutch of immediate personal, cultural and aesthetic problems in a new medium and within the confines of a plot which, if he were to remain faithful to the original, denies the easy resolution of the conflicts and questions the play raises. In this respect the play is perhaps best understood as a 'workshop' where the groundwork for a developing dramaturgy and feminist aesthetic is hammered out.

The unique, double-edged love which is central to *Antigone* holds a special fascination for Kennelly:

> In *Antigone*...I wanted to explore sisterhood, the loyalty a sister will show to a brother, against law, against marriage, against everything. There's no relationship like it; it has all the passion of your whole nature, this side of incest...it was a study of a girl all of whose impulses defied everything, in order to bury the boy, to give him dignity.[7]

Antigone's devotion to her slain brother Polyneices is blood-begotten, unconditional. It transcends and therefore must defy the man-made laws of the city-state; it is the root cause of the antagonism between herself and Creon. But there is another sibling relationship whose contours are more problematic. If the play has become an emblematic feminist text, its status as such is in part due to the ramifications of the disagreement between Antigone and Ismene. Their initial exchange summarises the issue which informs the action and defines the two polarised responses to Creon's decree in Antigone's radical defiance and Ismene's conservative compliance. Although the immediate frame of reference is local and familial, the larger, non-specific subject of their debate is, in effect, the position of women in the governance of the city state and, by extension, the amount of actual control they are free to exercise over their own

lives. Kennelly's diction makes it clear from the outset that Antigone
and Ismene are bound by a common 'curse'. Not only the stigma
attached to the house of Oedipus, a malaise which has brought
them 'shame, dishonour, ruin, pain' and lately left them 'robbed of
our two brothers', but their very womanhood, which renders them
powerless to counter Creon's despotism, makes them doubly afflicted.

As the children of Oedipus, and as women, the sisters appear
irrevocably fated. Yet Antigone and Ismene do not seem equally
oppressed by their femininity. For Ismene being female means (per-
haps as a matter of choice, certainly as a matter of course) being
marginalised, uninformed. As her first words reveal:

> Antigone, not a single word of friends,
> Not a single happy or miserable word,
> Has reached me...
> I might as well be dead
> Because I know nothing more,
> Not, as I have said, one solitary word.

Whereas Ismene has been kept, or has kept herself, well back from
the action, Antigone has been in the front lines, gathering inform-
ation, weighing the meaning and the consequences of Creon's 'word'.
Antigone's visit to Ismene is designed to test the latter's 'loyalty
and love', to determine whether she is 'of noble blood' or simply
'the slavish slut/ Of a noble line'. If Antigone's words are hard,
they are consonant with her attitude towards Ismene from the start.
Her tone is reproachful of Ismene's isolation, and is reciprocated
in Ismene's somewhat impatient description of Antigone as having
been 'broody and wild' from childhood. Kennelly's diction con-
notes intellectual introspection, maternal anxiety and independent
action, all characteristics Antigone possesses but which offend and
inhibit Ismene's less assertive sensibility. Antigone has brought
Ismene to a neutral zone, away from the male preserve of 'that
court of sinister stone'. Here, the sisters are on 'female ground'
and Ismene is free to think for herself. Her response to Antigone's
challenge to help bury Polyneices, if not what she hopes for, is
clearly what she expects. Ismene's assertion that they are 'mere
women' who must not 'disobey the word of Creon' makes her pos-
ition on the subordinate role of women, and therefore of Antigone's
threat to upset that order, perfectly apparent. For Ismene, the
authority of the state is paramount and she has neither the courage
nor the conviction to go against it. Antigone, on the other hand,
is not only unwilling but fundamentally unable to conform to the
prescriptions of what she sees as an unjust law. Her loyalty is not

to 'the ambitious living' but 'the mistreated, noble dead'. In choosing 'love' over 'frustration' she credits 'those laws/ Established in honour by the gods'. The law Antigone is talking about pre-dates and, in her view, transcends civil law: it is the law of kinship, which entails allegiance to a chthonic, intuitive, irrational but deeply religious sense of justice which is the inverse of Creon's rationalist meting of reward and punishment. Thus when Antigone speaks of her 'strength' as her most vital resource, what she means is the mental and spiritual conviction which keeps her sensitive to this knowledge. The case for civil disobedience as the 'right' reaction to self-aggrandising totalitarianism is virtually conceded in this opening exchange. Despite her departing reminder that 'Those who love you/ Will always hold you dear', the majority of modern productions impress that Ismene embodies the reactionary, visionless outlook of the status quo, in especial the sensible, even-minded women upon whom the state relies for its tacit support.

Kennelly's version is less single-minded in this respect. Without disturbing either the semantic richness or the political incisiveness of Sophocles, he manages to focus our attention first and foremost on the relationship between Antigone and Ismene as sisters and as women, and only secondarily on their function as the representatives of private and public interests, left- and right-wing thinking. We are made fully aware of the deep familial wounds which bind them, of their very different natures and, consequently, of the antagonisms which divide them. While he cannot but champion Antigone's heroic efforts, Kennelly is equally sympathetic to both sisters and is careful to emphasise that each is suppressed by Creon's strictures. he is at pains to draw out the tension between the sisters' love for one another and the difficulties they as women encounter in the political arena, and in turn to set that aspect of 'sisterhood' against Antigone's feelings about Polyneices. In seeking to define 'love', the question Kennelly asks is not which kind of love is greater – sister for sister, sister for brother – but how they are different, and what that difference tells us about human nature in general, and love in particular. He does this through a use of language which is direct and simple, yet emotive and poetically intricate. The dynamics of the sisters' relationship is conveyed through carefully modulated diction and intonation, which in turn directs us toward the issue of language and its centrality in the play.

Virginia Woolf was among the first feminist theorists to suggest that woman experience, think and therefore write the world differently from men.[8] The relevance of this proposition to Kennelly's

Antigone is worth pointing out: the exchange between Antigone and Ismene is essentially about correlations between language and gender, and so prepares us for Antigone's struggle towards 'articulate action'. Their debate is peppered with references to the power of language, from the initial allusion to the curse on the house of Oedipus through to Antigone's oath to make good her promise to bury her brother. The term 'word' is uttered no fewer than twenty times in the first 160 lines, and Kennelly's choice of repetition over variation is indicative of the weight he attaches to it.

While the play's primary conflict is between the power of authority invested in Creon's word and Antigone's bid to affirm that her promise is equally valid and right, the more subtle clash is between masculine and feminine discourse, between gendered ways of seeing and saying the world. Whereas Creon's language is the unequivocal and, as the chorus argues, necessarily uncompromising voice of effective government, the issue is complicated, and the drama enriched, by the fact that we are presented with at least two models of feminine discourse: Ismene's traditional posture of submissive silence and Antigone's vigorous challenge to patriarchy. The latter's 'cold words' are as rigid as Creon's, but with the difference that they involve the struggle for a language which fits her experience and her beliefs. Thus the question which becomes central to Kennelly's, as to any feminist, interpretation of the play is not simply which sister's stance is preferable, but which is in fact possible. The import of this opening section is succinctly summarised by Roche:

> The first scene between the sisters establishes a sense of woman not only taking over the moral vacuum left by men but transforming the image of heroism from violent self-assertiveness to ministering self-sacrifice. [9]

What follows is a development of this difference – the feminine alternative – via the enlargement of Kennelly's focus on gender and language. Each scene exposes the layers and ambiguities of the feminine incarnate in Antigone and her word made action.

Learning that someone has observed the rites he has outlawed, Creon is infuriated. In his ensuing tirade he twice reveals the unconscious assumption that such an act is beyond the province of any woman: 'What *man* alive would dare to do this thing?' and later, 'If you don't find the *man* who buried Polyneices/…You will be strung up alive' (*my emphasis*). The same dramatic irony informs the vocabulary of the chorus' second ode, beginning as it does with the celebrated lines 'Wonders are many/ And none is more wonderful than man'. Here too Kennelly exercises stark incremental repetition to underscore that, even as a candidate for the most marginalised of creatures, woman does not qualify in the popular imagination (again, the italics are mine here):

Whoever dishonours the laws of the land,
Scorns the justice loved by the gods,
That *man* has no city,
That *man* must live where no one lives.
Never may he visit my home,
Never share my thoughts.
That *man* must know his madness is his own
And is not part of the people.
He is a severed limb,
A severed head
Unacceptable to the conscious living
And the restful dead.

The impact of the guard's revelation that Antigone, a 'mere girl', is the malefactor leaves the chorus stunned, Creon 'doubly-insulted'. The avian imagery which studs his report of her discovery sets Creon's curses 'Beating like the wings of maddened birds/ About to swoop and rip my brains and heart out' against Antigone's maternal rage. Whereas Creon's threats carry the weight of imminent punishment, Antigone's pain renders her all but inarticulate, grasping for another means of pronouncing her sorrow:

I saw this girl. She gave a sharp cry
Like a wounded bird or a mother
Brutally stripped of her children.
When she saw the corpse deprived
Of the covering dignity of dust,
She cried a cry beyond all bounds of words
And cursed whoever did that deed.

The association of pathetic fallacy with Antigone's retreat from language is followed by a crucial exchange in which Creon addresses her in blatantly sexist terms. However, her immediate, subversive response marks a recovery of language and a recognition that she must learn to use it in her own way and to achieve her own ends:

CREON. You, *girl*, staring at the earth,
    Do you admit, or do you deny,
    This deed?
ANTIGONE. (*Looking up.*) I admit it, *man*.

Antigone's challenge to Creon's masculine ethos is double-edged. When she asserts 'Word and deed are one in me./ That is my glory' and goes on to disclose that the people in fact support her but are silent in fear of Creon's reaction, she threatens not just to undermine the basis of his authority and power, but to equal and possibly surpass his perceived sexual superiority as well. In short, Antigone implies that she will live as a man, something Creon fails to tolerate or understand: 'I would be no man,/ She would be the man/ If I let her go unpunished'.

In aligning herself with the non-secular otherworld of the gods, the underworld of the dead, Antigone seeks to counter hatred with love, to reinstate the non-patriarchal, alternative values of blood and family in place of the interventionist laws of the city-state. So complete is her commitment that she has chosen martyrdom over betrayal. As she reminds Ismene, 'I chose to die for love', 'My life is an act of service to the dead'. Yet however independent, her defiance is also an arguably self-interested gesture. For in her admonition of Ismene – 'There were two worlds, two ways./ One world approved your way,/ The other, mine' – and later the chorus – 'You know all about men...power...money...But you know nothing of women' – Antigone reveals what amounts to a personal religion which is prototypically feminist in premise and mode. For while she may oppose Creon on his own ground, 'as a man', she does not renounce her femininity; on the contrary, she pushes ever more deeply into that paradoxically new yet familiar territory where identity and sexuality are coterminous. Indeed, so unique is her venture that it carries her beyond the experience of either sex: 'I am a woman without fear/ In a hole in the rocks/ Where no man or woman dare venture'. Yet as a woman, Antigone is unaccustomed to such control and responsibility, and the prospect of self-creation is frightening, something which would choke her 'like a chicken-bone/ Stuck in my throat...Like ivy choking a house'. Trepidation, however, rapidly reverts to conviction, so much so that she can make the quasi-hubristic claim 'If I lived,/ I could change all the men of the world'.

The magnitude of the individual and the institution she is up against is fully exposed in Creon's treatment of Antigone and Ismene, and in particular of his own son, Haemon. His 'advice' to Haemon quickly degenerates into a diatribe in which women like Antigone are denounced as 'treacherous' and 'disobedient', and sons instructed not to think for themselves but 'Obey [their] father's will in everything'. This oration is symptomatic of his fear of being shamed by a woman – 'If I must fall from power/ Let it be by a man's hand,/ Never by a woman's'. Haemon's temperate appeal for a more democratic, pluralist, feminised form of government meets with a predictable rebuke: 'You would put a man below a woman...

Go be a woman/ Since you understand the thing so well'. We are returned to Antigone's words to the chorus which, in the light of Haemon's predicament, remind us of the difficulties involved in making a place for women in established male-centred codes:

What man
Knows anything of women?

If he did
He would change from being a man
As men recognise a man.

Finally imprisoned in 'the loneliest place in the world...a hole among the rocks', Antigone has made, it seems, the highest sacrifice, exchanging marriage and children for a tomb.

The physical immediacy of her oblation links her 'body language' to accepted notions about the necessarily corporeal, non-literate nature of female creativity and self-expression, as well as bringing it into line with the intuitive, emotive sphere she represents. By the same token, however, it identifies female creativity – Antigone's 'word' – solely with female sexuality. Her individual protest is ironically overcome by her gender, and the gap between male and female remains unbridgeable. To see Antigone's tragic victory in this way is to concede that because she is a 'mere woman' she cannot, nor should she ever presume to, achieve the autonomy she seeks, or address Creon in a language which is 'sexually pluralist' and therefore politically effective.

Antigone's solitary courage *does* make her an exemplary woman ahead of her time, but the 'body language' she uses to state her case, and to achieve what measure of revenge she can, is in fact a non-language. The audience is made to question the masculine hierarchy Creon stands for, but at the price of Antigone's silence. 'If I lived I would change all men.' *If* she lived. Within the parameters of the play, however, her declamatory gesture dies with her and she remains a victim, compelled in her death to share the silence Ismene recommends in the opening scene. Where Antigone's language survives, of course, is in each new performance of the play.

I suggested earlier that Kennelly's *Antigone* is a 'workshop' for both his move towards writing for the stage and the development of a feminist aesthetic. In terms of imagery, diction and characterisation, it is obviously connected to his poetry; in terms of issues and concerns it strikes out more forcefully than he had previously done at the oppressive forces of patriarchy in contemporary, particularly Irish, society in the seventies and eighties. As Kennelly shapes it, *Antigone* becomes a cautionary tale of sorts, warning both the Creons and the Antigones (whether we understand them in socio-political or psycho-sexual terms) in his audiences against the dangers, in the first instance, of denying the feminine, and in the second, of 'excessive love', of making 'too great a sacrifice' and an end in silence. Kennelly's *Antigone is* a play for and about women. Not only does it give Irish women a voice familiar in idiom and interest, but alongside caution it offers encouragement, finding in Antigone a model for the strength and conviction required to be 'mistress of your own fate', the author of your own language. The black hole Antigone must descend into is on one level an emblem of annihilating silence. But on another it represents the next stage on the journey towards 'articulate action' which is the destiny of all the Antigones we encounter in Kennelly's writing. Without that descent we would not have the voices of Medea and Hecuba and Cassandra or Lorca's Spanish wives and widows, for it is in this darkness that Kennelly has listened most intently to women as they learn to rage.

Extract from Kathleen McCracken's essay 'Rage for a New Order: Brendan Kennelly's Plays for Women', in *Dark Fathers into Light: Brendan Kennelly*, edited by Richard Pine (Bloodaxe Books, 1994).

NOTES:

1. George Steiner, *Antigones* (Oxford: Clarendon Press, 1984), p.138.
2. Anthony Roche, 'Ireland's *Antigone*: Tragedy North and South', *Cultural Contexts and Literary Idioms in Contemporary Irish Literature*, edited by Michael Kenneally (Gerrards Cross: Colin Smythe, 1988), pp.221-50.
3. Roche, p.246.
4. Kennelly, 'Learning From Our Contradictions', *Ireland: Look, The Land Is Bright* (Ireland Funds Conference Proceedings, 1990), p.23.
5. Steiner, p.231 ff.
6. Steiner, p.150.
7. Kennelly, 'Q. & A. with Brendan Kennelly', with Richard Pine, *Irish Literary Supplement*, 9.1 (Spring 1991), p.22.
8. Virginia Woolf, *A Room of One's Own* (1929; New York: Harcourt, Brace, Jovanovich, 1981), pp.97-104.
9. Roche, p.242.

EURIPIDES'
MEDEA

A NEW VERSION

for Susan Curnow & Ray Yeates

PREFACE

In 1985 I submitted a version of Sophocles' *Antigone* to the Abbey Theatre in Dublin. The play was produced in 1986 at the Peacock, to mixed reviews. One evening in the theatre, a member of the audience, a woman, walked up to me and said, 'You understand women's rage. Do *Medea* next. Many people say the play is about jealousy. It's not, it's about rage. Do it.' Having said that, the woman walked away from me. Her words stuck.

This may be as appropriate a moment as any to say that most of the insights about life and literature I've picked up from people, rather than from my own attempts to think, have come from women. And this learning has happened in the most casual ways, just like that little encounter in the Peacock Theatre. As far as I'm concerned, women have a way of saying perceptive things that is very different from men. They talk to me at times as if they'd been thinking for quite a while about the particular matter that's puzzling me; then they say whatever they've got to say candidly and simply and, to my mind, unforgettably. From their tone of simplicity and candour, I can tell that they're worth listening to, and worth following. Why are the words of complete strangers so compelling? Why do they make coherent and lucid what I'd been clumsily and blindly trying to come to grips within myself? The old term "women of the streets" has a very special and valuable meaning for me. Somehow or other, certain women, when they decide to do so, get to the core of almost any matter touching on feelings much more precisely, and with an astounding mixture of sensitivity and something approaching an unemphatic brutality, than most men are capable of doing, or even seem to wish to do.

Dublin is a city of maliciously wagging tongues. It is also a city where unsolicited help and illumination can come your way, if you learn to listen. Stabs in the back are often compensated for by wise, kind words to your face. The air is a fascinating blend of poison and good will.

I spent the best part of the summer of 1986 in St Patrick's Psychiatric Hospital in Dublin. It was, on the whole, a fine summer although a very fierce storm hit Dublin in August, causing the river Dodder to overflow and flood many homes in the Ballsbridge area of the city. I was trying to recover from prolonged alcoholism and I found myself listening, listening, especially to women. The women I listened to ranged in age from about seventeen to about seventy. Many of them had one thing in common.

Rage. Rage mainly against men, Irishmen like myself. As I listened day after day and night after night to these women talking about men I'd never met, but whom I could recognise in myself, I became aware of the fact that a major reason for their rage was because they were more *conscious* than the men they'd lived with, or left, or been jilted or betrayed or beaten up by. Sometimes these women, these "sick" or "mentally unbalanced" or "mad" women, couldn't fully articulate their feelings about men; but when they could their words were often savage and pitiless and precise. Some of them seemed to me to be unutterably hurt. But even more than that, they were conscious of the hopeless gulf between them and the men they described as cocky, self-indulgent, plausible 'masters' of the house and the pub, the club and the bookie's office, the street and the bed. The rage of these women was the rage of people who'd been used and abused over the years by men who quite often didn't even visit them in hospital. This was the rage the woman who'd spoken to me in the Peacock Theatre a few months earlier had been talking about. This was the rage that I tried to present in *Medea*, because that woman had told me I could. My little room in the hospital felt like a cell of rage. I wrote the first draft of the play in less than a month. I was in touch with that electricity which means that a play or poem goes a long way towards writing itself.

In 1983, I'd published *Cromwell*, a long poem about the man whose name still inspires eruptive hatred in Ireland. Early in 1984 I'd begun work on what was to become *The Book of Judas*, an epic poem trying to deal with betrayal and related matters in history and myth as well as in various kinds of human relationships. My mind was preoccupied with what I called Judasanity, the alternative 'Christianity' that is frequently and widely practised in Ireland, but which insists on not recognising itself for what it is. These women in hospital, expressing their rage at betrayal and violence and cruel indifference, entered *The Book of Judas*. And many themes and preoccupations, even obsessions, in *The Book of Judas* spilled into the rage and accusations of *Medea*. Across cultures, across the centuries, feelings, words and images began to fertilise each other. This kind of cross-fertilisation proves and underlines the delusions, the true madness inherent in that purely chronological view of reality beloved of minds that often condemn the kind of "madness" I met in these women in St Patrick's. (Did the bold St Patrick ever realise what he was giving his name to?).

In turning to Euripides' great play, I knew I was meeting a woman who, among other things, had deceived her father and murdered her brother, to flee with Jason. She gave all, and expected the same. She

71

was magical, lethal, loving, a sorceress, a barbarian, and had a savage truthfulness in her heart. Euripides presents her as an abandoned, betrayed woman bent on revenge; he also brilliantly suggests the twisted consequences of that revenge. Medea is transfigured into an almost superhuman destroyer by her sense of wrong.

The Medea I tried to imagine was a modern woman, also suffering a terrible pain – the pain of consciousness of betrayal by a yuppified Jason, a plausible, ambitious, articulate and gifted opportunist who knows what he wants and how to get it. Medea, as I imagined her, plans to educate Jason in the consciousness of horror; she destroys his world but leaves him intact; and she instructs him very calmly and lucidly in the appalling consequences of this intactness. All his opportunistic genius for getting a grip on things, for exploiting his macroview of circumstances, now becomes the instrument to lacerate and torment his deepening consciousness of deepening loss. Medea, as I see her, inflicts on Jason the ultimate cruelty: she sentences him to life. This play ends with a cool, horrific talk between two people who, in their different ways, must live with themselves. One senses, however, that this is going to be somewhat harder for Jason.

Medea, when produced, got the sorts of responses that showed its ability to stir very differing and contradictory emotions in people. Most women were moved by it; I received many letters which echoed Medea's feelings about Jason. Some women thought the play was a diatribe against women, the work of a woman-hater who didn't recognise his own hate. Many men didn't like it, felt accused by it, thought it unfair, showing 'only one side of the story'. A few men told me they were grateful for it. One man said I was a bitter bitch in disguise. What disguise, I wonder?

It is true that we disguise ourselves in various ways. *Medea* is a play in which disguises are ripped away. When that happens, the reader and the audience will see what they are, or are not prepared, to see; what they choose or dare to see; and having seen it, what they permit themselves to remember. I remember women, their honest, bitter words in a most humane hospital, talk of a bad storm hitting the city outside, and myself imagining a devastating woman in a cell of rage.

I would like to thank Neil Astley for his excellent suggestions concerning the final shape of this text on the page, and for the note opposite.

BRENDAN KENNELLY
April 1991

MEDEA AND JASON

Medea was a sorceress and priestess of Hecate, the niece of Circe, and daughter of Aeetes, king of Colchis (son of Helios, the Sun god). When Jason came to Colchis with the Argonauts in his quest for the Golden Fleece, Hera caused Aphrodite to make Medea fall violently in love with him, and in exchange for a promise of marriage she helped him overcome the trials devised by her father as a condition for winning the Fleece. Realising that Aeetes meant to kill the Argonauts in the night, Medea warned them and led Jason to the Fleece. During their escape her half-brother Apsyrtus was murdered: some sources claim she dismembered him and left the pieces to delay her father's pursuit; others that she tricked him into a meeting with Jason, who killed him.

Jason was a celebrated hero, the son of Aeson, who should have been king of Iolchos after the death of his father Cretheus. But his uncle Pelias usurped the throne, and Jason's mother arranged for him to be raised in safety by the centaur Chiron. When Jason returned to Iolchos to claim his inheritance, Pelias agreed to resign if he would recover the Golden Fleece, the skin of a miraculous winged ram which had rescued his cousins Helle and Phryxus after their father Athamas had been tricked into sacrificing them to the gods: Helle fell from the ram's back and was drowned in the sea, while Phryxus reached Colchis where he sacrificed the ram to Zeus, and was befriended and then killed by King Aeetes, Medea's father, who kept the Golden Fleece.

When Jason and Medea arrived in Iolchos with the Fleece, Medea claimed she could rejuvenate the old by cutting them up and boiling them in a magic potion, and urged the daughters of Pelias to help her make him young again. The daughters obliged, chopping up their father while he was in a drugged sleep, but Medea disappeared once he was in the pot, and with no magic spell to transform him the usurper was turned into stew instead. Jason's people were so outraged by this that the couple were forced to flee to Corinth, where they lived for ten years, until Jason deserted Medea for King Creon's daughter Glauce. Euripides' play *Medea* tells the story of that betrayal and her revenge. After her flight, she married Aegeus, King of Athens, but was banished by him when she tried to poison his long lost son Theseus. She returned to Colchis, where some sources say she was reconciled with Jason. After her death she married Achilles in the Elysian Fields. Jason was later killed when a piece of his ship fell on top of him.

MEDEA

Brendan Kennelly's *Medea* was first performed by the Medea Theatre Company in the Dublin Theatre Festival at the Royal Dublin Society Concert Hall on 8 October 1988. It was revived on 6 July 1989 at the Gate Theatre, Dublin, prior to a tour of England which took in the Purcell Room at London's South Bank Centre. The cast at the first performance was as follows:

NURSE	Stella McCusker
TEACHER	Geoff Golden
CHORUS	Aine Ní Mhuirí
MEDEA	Susan Curnow
CREON, *King of Corinth*	Liam O'Callaghan
JASON	Michael James Ford
AEGEUS, *King of Athens*	Christopher Casson
MESSENGER	Poll Moussoulides
CHILDREN *of Medea*	Brian Hickey
	Dean Clifford
CREON'S GUARDS	Shay Dunphy
	William Cunningham
DIRECTOR	Ray Yeates
ASSISTANT DIRECTOR	John Breen
DESIGNERS	Chisato Yoshimi
	Katrina McKillen
LIGHTING DESIGN	Bernard Griffin
MUSIC COMPOSER	Noel Eccles
MUSIC PERFORMER	Paul Maher
STAGE DIRECTOR	Marie Breen
ADMINISTRATOR	Arthur Duignan
PRESS OFFICER/PRO	Julie Barber
PHOTOGRAPHS	Tom Lawlor

The play is set outside Medea's house in Corinth.

PART ONE

NURSE. Glory to Heaven for home and family:
   a man, a woman, children.
   Medea left her home
   for love of Jason,
   seeker of the Golden Fleece.
   Why must a man be always seeking something?
   Why must a woman seek a man who seeks his special gold?
   Seeking! Seeking! That's the curse and glory of our kind.
   But what do we find?
   Medea did everything for Jason,
   left her home and country for him,
   cared for him, loved him, reared his children.
   But Jason betrayed her, took another woman.
   Medea's love is hatred now.
   Jason has betrayed
   his children by Medea, to sleep
   with a woman of royal blood, the daughter
   of Creon who is the ruler of our people.
   Medea cannot believe
   Jason's treachery, his ambitious lechery.
   Kings will be strong on thrones
   if they are uppermost in bed.
   People are ever eager to believe
   what randy kings have said.
   (Pause.)
   My mistress and her children
   have been betrayed by Jason,
   the celebrated seeker of the Golden Fleece.
   Betrayal is the ripest crop in this land.
   The more it is slashed, the stronger it grows.

   Ever since Medea heard
   of Jason's treachery, she has lain prostrate
   on the earth itself, a womanbody of grief,
   shrinking with ceaseless tears. Her eyes
   are riveted on the clay, as if
   she knew that nothing lives above the grass.
   Her soul is hurt. She will not listen
   to the words of friends, as if these words
   were the stupid croaking of crows
   in the sky that is more meaningless than dust.
   Sometimes, however, she shifts her neck,
   her beautiful neck.

Talking clearly to herself, in grief,
about her father and her country and her home –
the home she betrayed to come here
with Jason, who left her in complete contempt,
although she'd left her country for him.
Medea – now Medea knows what it means
to leave a land where there is love
for her in people's eyes,
to live in a country where eyes are cold
with neglect, indifference and contempt.
Medea lives among the faces of an arrogant land.
Arrogance is the inspiration of hatred
and – the gods be with us – she has begun
to hate her own children, the very sight of them.
They are sprung of the seed of Jason,
seeker of the Golden Fleece.
The Golden Fleece, indeed!
Can any man or God tell me
what is the Golden Fleece?
The shearings of a sheep, or sly,
alluring threads of gold?
Whatever Jason seeks – Medea hates.
(Pause.)
When I see her prostrate on the earth
I know she is drinking the knowledge of the evil dead,
the fiery strength of poisoned spirits,
the secrets of malignant centuries.
What is growing, this very moment,
in her prostrate mind?
Even as a girl, Medea had a dangerous
way of thinking about herself and others.
She will tolerate no hurt or harm to her heart.
I know Medea. She frightens me.
She is prostrate now, but when she rises from the earth
she may steal into the palace
where Jason lies, drive a sword
into his heart, his belly, chop
his penis and his testicles for the pure pleasure of revenge.
So there lies Jason of the Golden Fleece!
Fleece is what he sought, blood is what he found.
(Pause.)

Among women, Medea has the most cunning mind of all.
She is fox and badger, ferret and stoat,
eagle and hawk.
She can master seven kinds of talk,
using the same words.
She is the clouds the sun cannot penetrate,
she is the sun the clouds cannot resist,
she is the voices of the rain,
she is the silence of an unread book,
she has a tongue to flay anyone who
bandies words with her. Those who
feel the lash of that tongue take
a long time to heal. A few have
never found the cure. The day may come again
when she'll be as fierce and deadly
as she seems broken now.

Enter TEACHER *and* BOYS.

Here come the children
from their play, free of the thoughts
that make their mother prone with hurt
and anger on the earth, as if she cannot
wait to become part of it. Such thoughts
are far from children's playful hearts.

TEACHER. Why are you standing alone at the gate,
muttering to yourself? Where is Medea?
Why are you not with her?

NURSE. Medea's sorrow is so deep,
so driven into the earth, I
had to come out to tell the wind
and sun, to tell the patient, listening sky
itself, the story of her sorrow.

TEACHER. Is Medea still crying?

NURSE. Medea's grief is only starting.
Her tide of bitter sorrow is only
at its source.
                    She is prostrate now.
When she is upright, let Jason be careful.

TEACHER. Medea knows nothing
of what is in store for her.

NURSE. What?

TEACHER. Certain things must not be said.

NURSE. Out with it, old man.
(*Pause.*)
Speak, or die accursed.

TEACHER. I walked beside the sacred waters
where the old men sit and talk
(in mockery or affection I know not).
These old men look like scruffy, mocking prophets.
As I passed, one of them
laughed aloud,
saying that Creon,
ruler of this country,
planned to expel Medea and her children
from this clean city
back to her own stinking land.
Creon, the old man said, held that
Medea, a cunning woman,
and her little brats
were not worthy to live
in this fair land he rules.
Pollution, he said, takes many forms,
and woman is the worst.
Her stink is natural and inevitable,
the hot, strong stink of a roused, prowling cat.
She uses perfume and powder to conceal it
but most of all, she uses cunning.
I am a teacher, I know boys and girls.
I know that Creon's words are lies
but I dare not say so in public.

NURSE. Will Jason allow his children
to be pitched into exile?

TEACHER. Old loves are graves,
new loves grow out of rotting corpses.
To Jason, Medea's love is dead,
a lost excitement buried in the past.

NURSE. Our lives are finished here.
The shame of exile is the worst of all.
An exile belongs nowhere, his name is nothing,

his memory is scurrilous and impoverished
he is the true outsider because he is outside
himself, the little quiet
familiar things that make his soul.
If Creon sends us into exile,
he puts in exile all our souls.
Exile is the worst form of living death.

TEACHER No sermons on exile, my dear.
Keep quiet. Not another word.
This is no time for Medea to hear your grisly story.

NURSE. (*To the* CHILDREN.)
Do you see what your father is doing to you?
Because your father is my master, I cannot wish
him dead, but he is showing
the most callous hatred
to you, the children of his blood,
who should be one
with the beat of his heart.
This cannot be natural.
Where is your father's love for you?

TEACHER. Do you not realise that people love themselves
more than anyone else in the world?
Is there one person in this city today,
in this house tonight,
who can swear he loves his neighbour
more than himself? That is not to say
love does not exist, shyly, in the hearts
of men and women. And yet, my experience
as a teacher of boys and girls
tells me they love themselves more than others,
rehearsing to become decent men and women,
respectable, house-owning, careful,
somewhat ulcerous perhaps,
threatened with (let's say) angina,
that sweaty tightening of the chest,
that chilling of the hands and feet.
Consider one such man. In a gesture of defiance
against himself and what he stands for,
he becomes, one summer evening, a little tipsy.
There grows in him a strange compulsion

to spill his little, hidden agonies
into the ear of a twitching stranger
who has left his wife and children
for reasons that he tries to drown in a glass,
seeing himself risking a thrilling freedom
in some hallucinating city of the future.
But come, I am frogleaping the centuries.
Still, that is a teacher's privilege –
the one inspiring madness his profession allows –
the knowledge that all things happen at the same time,
to the same people (though they all die)
as the centuries flow by, smiles upon their lips
at the spectacle of honest, helpless repetition.
It is a simple tale. People love themselves
as they sense they should.
Failing in this, they invent a successful god
and plague him with their failures.

NURSE. (*To the* CHILDREN.)
     Inside. Inside with you!
     (*To the* TEACHER.)
     Keep these children as far from Medea
     as you possibly can. Don't let them come
     within an inch of their mother
     especially when that icy anger freezes her eyes
     and freezes all within the orbit of her rage.
     Because of that rage, people will die.
     May it be her enemies that die, not her friends.

MEDEA. (*Within.*) Grief!
     I curse this life of grief and pain
     heaped on me by the man
     that I created with my blood
     until he thought he was a god.
     His love was life to me.
     It is an insult now.

NURSE. (*To the* CHILDREN.)
     Dear children of my heart,
     your mother's heart
     is troubled beyond words, her
     anger is a storm in her blood.
     So quick, quick, children, hurry indoors
     as quickly as you can. Above all don't

go near her, don't let her fix
her eyes on you, her kiss
is deadly, her caress
a warm poison. Her touch is
gentle, but her will is iron.
Go on, my children, go indoors,
be quick. Quick.

The CHILDREN *leave with* TEACHER.

(*Pause.*)
                              Soon Medea's
grief will burst over this
world in a never-before-known storm
of rage. Men will have forgotten
the name of peace. Has peace a name?
Will Medea destroy the name of peace
and put a fake word in its place?
Will the real word be destroyed
by Medea's rage? Is this her
rage – to falsify all words, so that
men and women, in their talk,
are capable of nothing but lies?

Is her rage directed against
children learning words, against
the wordless child in the womb? Has
Medea made women the carriers of liars?
And what is Medea, fierce, true,
trusting, self-willed Medea, to do
with men-liars, child-liars,
liars unborn?
                              Will Medea allow
child-liars grow up to be
father-liars who will beget child-liars, who will
become father-liars to beget child-liars? Only
the earth is true, we must shelter
ourselves from it, protect our
valuable lies as we protect our
children, clothe them, teach
them to communicate. Insure them.
Educate them. Bless them. Send them out
into the world to bring new children
to the earth. The world of rage.

Medea's world. The world of rage.
World without lies. Well-dressed lies.
Stylish lies. Legal lies. Family lies.
Religious lies. Politicians' lies.
Writers' lies. Theatre lies.
Actors' lies. Audiences' lies.
Critics' lies. Husbands' lies. Poets' lies.
Judges' lies. Wives' lies. Girls' lies. Teachers' lies.
Doctors' lies. Lovers' lies. Kings' lies.
The lies of writing about lies.
The lies of words. The lie that is
at the heart of all lies –
the truth, and the hot-faced seekers
after truth. The lies of those who
think they have cut the lies out of their hearts,
the lies of hearts who think they are the sole
possessors of the truth.

MEDEA. (*Within.*) Wronged, wronged, I am wronged
in every deepest corner of my being.
My sons, your father hates me
and every day you live is but a curse.
May death sweep your father
and sweep you too, my children,
and sweep away to blackest hell
every trace and sign
of this accursed family.

NURSE. Medea! Why do you bring
curses on your entire household?
Why will you make your sons
suffer for their father's sin? Why
must these innocent boys
bear the scourges of a guilty man?
(*Pause.*)
The souls of many kings and queens
are poisoned, vindictive to the end.
The more stylish their talk,
the more hardened their hearts.
They are made proud and pitiless
by their great reputations.
They are so used to giving commands
they cannot bear the thought of being checked.

This royal cocksureness will scorn all advice
though that advice be born of loving friendship.
It is more civilised
to live among your equals.
Your heart is more at ease.
I have no wish to be a sad old queen
shaking hands with every wide-eyed idiot
at some show or exhibition.
I'd prefer a pleasant, calm old age,
rocking gently with memories.
I pity royalty and its fatal obstinacy,
its fixed and stupid smile into the crushing mob,
its ludicrous elegance among the tatters,
its handsome hypocrisy, its descent
from murder, pillage, rapine, iniquity.
Mortals should practise moderation.
With moderation, old age can be a joy.

Enter CHORUS.

CHORUS. I heard a cry. It was
a woman's cry, fierce, piercing and demented
in the grip of some unbearable pain.
It was Medea's cry – no woman
ever cried like Medea. It is like
the cry of Nature itself, the cry of creatures
losing their young in the wilderness, the cry
of a woman who knows she has a dead child
in her womb, the cry of the hare
when the hound's teeth sink into its neck.
But Medea's cry was deeper, purer, wilder
than any of these. It was the cry
of the first woman
betrayed by the first man.
It turned that very house into a cry.
That house is dear to my heart.
My heart echoes with Medea's cry.
She has my pity now, she always will.
I am loyal to her still.

NURSE. Jason's house was once a home.
It is a home no more.
The life has left it.
(*Pause.*)

Jason has a mistress in his bed
while Medea wastes away in her room.
Not a word of comfort can come
within a million moon-miles of her heart.

MEDEA. (*Within.*)   I want my brain
to be set on fire by a lightning-bolt from Heaven,
to burn out of my head those eyes
that have witnessed the treachery of men.
Men speak of good. Tell me, o tell me what is good?
Tell me, truly, what is the good of living?
I admit the hatred in my heart
for what I thought was good,
the pride and promise of those golden days.
I wished to live that promise without lies.
A lie is a kind of death. I will not continue
to live in this house of lies.

CHORUS. Medea, you are going mad with sadness,
your body is shrivelling at the thought
of another woman in your man's bed.
But why bother to lust for that particular bed?
Or are you so sick of living
that you cherish the thought of dying?
I pray you, do not pray for that.
Live, my dear Medea, live.
You are strong, imaginative, resourceful.
If your husband loves another woman,
that is a common thing. All over this city
men hurry to their lovers, or wait for them
where their beds are soft and warm,
where love can spend itself like any season,
can shed the guilt that is the enemy of love,
can kill the cold distance that makes
potential lovers strangers to each other.
This city is full of lovers, Medea.
It is also full of strangers.
Be a stranger if you will,
be a lover, if you can.
The man you believe you love is but one man.
Let no one man destroy your life.
This city teems with lovers. Find one.
Love him.

MEDEA. (*Within.*) Dear gods,
   I left my father, I killed my brother,
   I created my husband.
   My husband broke his oath.
   The answer is fire
   or the sword
   or the deadly wandering of poison
   in the guise of irresistible beauty.
   Beauty, poison, fire,
   fire that will be a rival to the sun,
   fire that will become a fire of legend
   because Jason broke the oath he made to me,
   to me, Medea.

NURSE. Medea knows the meaning of prayer.
   She knows the meaning of revenge. And she has
   schooled her heart in rage beyond my comprehension.

CHORUS. Whatever wisdom I possess is at her service.
   Nurse, I beg you bring her here, I beg you
   bring her out of that place. Tell her
   I am her friend. Hurry, before she wreaks
   havoc in the palace. There is no limit
   to the fury of such a sorrow, no
   boundary to the fierceness of such rage.

NURSE. I'll try, I'll try.
   She has a fierce look in her eyes,
   especially if she thinks you're going to speak to her.
   I think she thinks all human words are lies,
   that never again can any word be true.
   Her eyes rage: idiots and lunatics –
   that's the right name for poets
   who make up songs to celebrate
   the joy of life at feasts and banquets,
   but never have discovered a song or poem
   or music to rid the world
   of pain and sorrow, all the horrors
   that drive men and women to their graves.
   Music and poetry are pretty ornaments,
   trivial and attractive, but mere distractions
   from the wormy rot that waits us all.
   (*Pause.*)

I'll try to fetch Medea now.

NURSE *goes in.*

CHORUS. I hear a woman's cry of grief.
    She cries of misery, of bad luck,
    of the horrors of marriage, of broken
    oaths, of love betrayed.
    Every sound she utters is such
    a cry of grief, all language could be
    drowned in it. She makes me think that
    the saddest words are only a failure to cry.

Enter MEDEA.

MEDEA.
    (*To audience, looking also from time to time at the* CHORUS.)
    Women of this city,
    do not turn critical eyes on me.
    I have come out of that place.
    Your eyes are full of judgement
    but devoid of justice.
    He's a snob! She's a whore! He's a drunkard!
    I pitch judgement to the winds
    and cry for justice.
    I cry for justice though my life is over.
    It is the sweet taste of life I have lost,
    I who have tasted the sweetest moments life can offer,
    so sweet I knew they could not last.
    Sweetness is brief, bitterness is long.
    The man who was my world, my sun and moon and stars,
    my sacred rivers and holy mountains,
    has proved himself not a man, but a poisonous snake.
    And yet he feels and thinks,
    schemes, manipulates and plans,
    handles emotions as if they were money
    which he deposits safely in his pocket,
    fingering them for comfort or for fun.
    O yes, he feels and thinks.
    And yet, of all the creatures
    the fertile mind of Nature has conceived
    there are no creatures who can
    feel and think like women. That is why
    we are the unhappiest creatures

on the face of this creative earth.
First, all dressed in white, for the most part,
we are the playthings of men's bodies,
the sensual toys of tyrants.
Men, the horny despots of our bodies,
sucking, fucking, licking, chewing, farting into our skin,
sitting on our faces, fingering our arses,
exploring our cunts, widening our thighs,
drawing the milk that gave the bastards life.
And allowing for all that, there's another problem –
is he a good man or a bad?
Till the day he marries,
a man can conceal his true nature
by the careful exercise of style.
Style – that elegant lie.
After marriage, his true nature begins to emerge.
Marriage, happy, horrible, or dull, is revelation.
If separation follows, the woman
is often the object of sniggers,
the man, an object of sympathy.
If the marriage remains intact,
a woman needs second sight in order
to handle this stranger who is her
bedmate. What are his expectations,
his midnight tricks, his desires
to hurt or be hurt, his
terrified or savage ways, his
cold kindness, his savage
caresses, his lawful barbarisms,
the tragedy and comedy of
intercourse, his sudden loss of
interest in her body, his
turning his back on her as if
she didn't exist (does she? my friends)?
Does a woman really exist
apart from the "attention" a man
pays to her? Usually, this
"attention" happens in the warm
creaking of the bed, the rhythm
that leads to snores on one
side, and, often enough, tears
on the other. Tears and snores.

Silence and noise. Woman and man.
(*Pause.*)
It is often said that
we women have a comfortable life
in the safety of our homes, while
men go out to sweat at work,
or risk their lives in the terrible
dangers of war. Nonsense.
I'd rather sweat it out
in some stinking hellhole, or
fight a war in a foreign land
than give birth to a brat
who will add to the pollution
of this befouled earth
where even the seas are thick
with poison. However,
women of this city, you and I
are not in the same
position. This is your city.
You belong here.
You are here. Your friends are here.
You are comforted by familiar sights.
I, on the other
hand, am homeless, husbandless,
exiled and forsaken, wronged
by the man I loved, with
nobody to turn to in this
hour of cursed misfortune. Now,
dear sisters, dear women
with whom I have shared
my nightmare, there is one
thing I must ask of you.

If any punishment
falls on my husband's head, if he is
driven naked and lunatic
through the streets, screaming
obscenities most citizens
have never heard before
or even dreamed could
ever exist; if he should
lose what is nearest and
dearest to him in the world,

and storm demented
at the sight or thought
of unbearable loss,
tearing the flesh from
his own bones; then,
my sisters, I ask of you
only one thing: your silence.
Silence, the most powerful
weapon of all. We
women are known and proven
to be gentle, warm, considerate
creatures. But if there is
something terrible to be
done, a woman's
gentleness becomes the most
murderous weapon of all.
and it is all the more murderous
when the silence of women
surrounds the deed. That is why
I ask you all, here
and now, for the gift of your
silence. When I take revenge on Jason
let your silence be my strong approving witness.

CHORUS. Do as you will, Medea,
for your revenge is just,
your rage the cry for justice in your blood.
It is no wonder
that your blood cries out against injustice.
It is no wonder
that you would reduce your husband
and the woman in his bed
to ashes, and fling these ashes
wherever the winds may carry them.
But wait! Here comes Creon,
ruler of our land,
bristling with new plans.
Prepare to listen to a man.

Enter CREON.

CREON. I'm afraid of you.
You are a woman schooled in evil.
I am a man who senses evil, and is afraid of it.

You are maddened by the loss of your man's love.
Your eyes are burning pools of madness.
Evil seeps from every pore of your body.
I know about your threats to kill
bride, bridegroom and father of the bride.
Therefore, before you harm me and my kind,
I will harm you and yours.
You are to be driven into exile from my land,
You and your two sons. This exile will take place today.
Now. Without a single moment of delay. Without a word.
Get out of this land.

MEDEA. I am not an evil woman. I am a skilful woman.
Because I am skilful, I make distinctions.
Because I make distinctions, some people hate and fear me.
You say you are afraid of me.
Creon, my King and master, you have no need to fear me.
Fear the power of rumour, the envious blood,
the malignant energy of wagging tongues.
I was not born to harm great kings.
I hate my husband.
You have done no wrong against me,
yet you are afraid you will suffer
harm at my hands.
Why, in the name of all the gods, should I harm you?
You have exercised a father's right –
You have given your daughter
to the man you consider worthy.
That is natural, dignified, and proper.
How could I hate a man of such integrity?
Never.
It is my husband I hate.
(*Pause.*)
You are a wise king.
May the gods bless
every moment of your future,
but allow me and my two sons
to live in the shadow of the goodness of your rule.
If there is evil in me, it will be
driven into exile by your goodness and wisdom.
I have been foully used, but under you,
my King and master, that foulness will be dispelled,
and be replaced by good.

92

CREON. No! I cannot afford to listen to you.
    You have a tongue to make
    almost any man change his mind,
    but not Creon's mind, not the mind
    of the King of the people.
    Though there is praise and comfort in your words,
    they do not lessen the fear in my heart.
    In fact, I trust you now even less
    than when we began to speak.
    Your persuasiveness has increased my fear.
    (*Pause.*)
    It is easier for a man to defend himself
    against a hot-tempered woman
    than against a woman with an icy mind
    and a cool tongue. The most difficult
    obstacle of all is a woman's silence –
    it makes a man feel that his words are less
    than the squeaking of mice in the sleeping dark.
    So leave me now, and no more words.
    My mind is made up. Go, no more words.
    Your words of praise will turn
    to hate of me. I cannot listen.
    I *must* not listen. At this moment,
    I wish the gods would make me deaf.
    (*Pause.*)

MEDEA. Most royal and just of kings,
    I beseech you by your loving eyes
    on the young bride...

CREON. Your words are falling on deaf ears.
    You will never move me from my resolution.
    I will not be convinced by the words
    of a woman who has admitted
    hatred for her husband.

MEDEA. It is the truth. You are
    a known lover of the truth.

CREON. (*Pause.*) I love my family
    more than I love the truth.

MEDEA. The loves of men are sometimes a great evil.

CREON. Get out of my way, woman.
    Trouble me no more.

MEDEA. My troubles are my own.
My life is a list of troubles.

CREON. Throw her out.

MEDEA. No, not to be thrown out by servants.
I beg you, Creon –

CREON. Don't beg. Go.

MEDEA. I am ready to go.

CREON. Then why are you clutching me
so fiercely, as if you would
never let me go, as if you would
move me from my place?

MEDEA. I don't care
about myself, but I ask you to take
pity on the children. Creon, you
yourself are the kind father
of a princess. Kindness to children
is natural, the very sweetness
of the heart. Let me stay here
for one day to get myself and my children
ready for exile. Their father doesn't care,
so all the responsibility for our departure
falls on my shoulders.
I don't care about myself. It's
for my children I am crying now.
Mercy, Creon. Mercy for one day,
one last, loving, caring, crying day.

CREON. I know that I am making a mistake.
But let me give you one warning,
and one warning only.
If, when the sun rises tomorrow,
you and your children are found
within the boundaries of this land,
the three of you will die in that instant,
on that very spot.
You say I love the truth.
I have never spoken a truer word.
You may stay here for one day.
One day is not enough for you to do
what fills my heart and soul

94

with fear. One day, Medea, one day:
Do your work, then go your way.

Exit CREON.

CHORUS. Wretched Medea! Where will you go now?
    Is there, somewhere, a kindly
    stranger to take you in? Or
    will you become a muttering
    wanderer through unknown lands,
    a tattered, hungry beggar
    among strangers, at home in
    the dirt of the world, ignored
    by all but those with pity or
    contempt in their eyes? Nothing
    faces you but trouble. Trouble is
    your husband now.

MEDEA. Trouble? Nothing faces me but trouble?
    There's trouble ahead for the bride and groom,
    there's trouble ahead for Creon.
    Do you think I'd ever have spoken to the King just now
    if I were not sure of my own plans?
    If I were not sure of what I am going to do
    I would not have spoken to that fool
    nor clutched him, as he said, 'fiercely'.
    Men love to be held 'fiercely',
    it makes them think a woman weak.
    But Creon is such a fool,
    Such a victim of his own soft mercy,
    that though he might have spoiled my plans
    by shaming me into exile,
    he has allowed me one day,
    one sweet, vicious, vengeful, devastating day,
    to make three corpses –
    one of Creon, man of mercy,
    one of his daughter, thief of my man,
    one of my man, snake of my bed.
    He will be a living corpse.
    My sisters, I can think
    of many ways of ridding the world of these three.
    Fire appeals to me.
    So does the sword.
    Yet I believe I shall choose

the method for which I am most fitted.
Poison. Poison spreads slowly, unstoppably,
like the coming of a sick old age.
Think of poison spreading through
the bodies of lovers in the bridal bed.
The sort of poison I will inflict
will be deep and slow and constant
as the suffering I have endured.
There is nothing unfair in that.
Justice is granite.
All these days and nights when I cried and cried
something in me said
Justice will not be denied.
So, let me
imagine them dead. What city,
knowing the crime, would offer me
protection? Where can I be safe?
I must wait to carry out
the murders in secrecy. However,
if necessary, I shall do it
by the sword, and die, of course.
I don't fear that.

This is hard work. Hard work –
the source of all true happiness.
Never before
did I feel the fullness of womanhood,
the danger emanating with every breath.
It is exhilarating, irrepressible, new,
as though I were an army in myself.
Gentleness, timidity, have buried my ferocity.
What men call "charm" has quelled my real talent.

Betrayal has proved to me the evil of good men's consolation.
I am at home in my own evil.
It is the only force that brings justice
into this perfumed, jewelled, stylish world
of absolute injustice. A little poison,
properly administered, may restore the hope
of that lost justice that compelled us
to give respect to others, and dignity
to the mind of man. A little poison
may perform the miracle.

CHORUS. The rivers of the world
        have turned round, flown against themselves
        to find their origins. They defy the laws
        that make them flow naturally to the sea.
        The earth, and the moral laws that
        help to keep the world beautiful
        and fertile, have entered a most
        destructive madness. Treachery
        and betrayal have gripped the hearts
        of men, so that they sneer
        at Heaven's laws. But there will
        come a change, the voice of
        Heaven will be heard, and
        the true glory of women will
        enrich the centuries, kind wisdom
        echoing down the ages as
        the unpolluted river sings itself
        forward in joyous fluency
        to the sea. With equal joyous fluency,
        the time is coming when honour
        will be paid to women, when
        their feelings will not be made
        by men, when slavery will not
        masquerade as love, when
        a man's tone of voice will not
        create a tremor in a woman's
        reply, when a woman will
        not live to please
        an inferior man, when a woman
        will not sit in silence while
        her master broods in sullen
        superiority, when decisions
        are her agreement to his
        suggestions, when her hate
        can show itself, articulate
        and pure. Then, too, the
        shadow of justice may be
        thrown across the earth,
        like a warm coat across
        the shoulders of a shivering beggar.

        There will be songs
        to celebrate the terrible truth

of women. There will be
womansongs in answer to the false
songs of men.

You, Medea, you
woman among women,
left your father's home
to live in a foreign land.
Tonight, your bed is empty, your
lover a bitter memory, you are
a wretched woman, nothing faces you
but exile. Yet, Medea,
you are a true woman, one
who is not "civilised" by men,
a woman not moulded
by weaklings who are so afraid
of women they must show
their superiority, their indolent
or furious strength, their
"manhood". "Manhood."

A hood worn over
the head of a man so that he
cannot see, so that he
can be wilfully blind.
Pity the man who does not question his manhood.
Manhood is not instinctive strength.
Manhood is deliberate blindness.

Deliberate blindness
will not be true to oaths. Deliberate
blindness has nothing but contempt
for honour. Honour is outraged
and has taken refuge in the clouds. Medea,
you know where you stand.
Woman among women, you cannot
return to your father's house, you
are alone, and another woman,
a princess, has stolen
your husband, shares his bed,
and taken your place. That is
who you are, Medea, in this world of men.

Enter JASON.

JASON. I have frequently observed
    that an intractable woman
    is impossible to handle.
    She is incapable of listening to reason
    and resorts to loud, incessant cursing
    as though she were unaware
    of the infinite possibilities of that civilised language
    which has taken centuries to render
    logical and lucid.
    When you might have held your tongue
    and spoken in a fit way to your superiors,
    your words were barbarous and arrogant.
    Your savage language has guaranteed your exile.
    Had you exercised discretion you would be safe.
    The only mastery you have is of abuse.
    Not that your abuse troubles *me* in the slightest.
    Continue saying that Jason is the basest of men.
    But as for your abuse of royalty, know
    you are lucky that exile is
    your only punishment. I spent a lot
    of time persuading Creon to allow
    you to stay in this land. But,
    obstinate woman, you simply kept on
    abusing the king. That is why
    your vile and poisoned tongue will send you into exile.
    You'd have been a happy woman
    if you'd been born without a tongue in your head.
    In spite of that, I have come here
    to offer money to you and the children.
    Exile is hard, and very expensive.
    I know you hate me with all your heart.
    I cannot think of you with cruelty.
    Please accept my offer of money
    and of whatever help you need.
    I will give you what I can.
    (*Pause.*)

MEDEA. Stink of the grave, rot of a corpse's flesh,
    slime of this putrid world,
    unburied carcase of a dog in the street,
    the black-yellow-greeny spit of a drunk at midnight –
    these are my words for you.

You dare to come to me, my worst enemy.
You know this is not bravery,
not generosity,
but the triumphant ugliness
on the face of a traitor,
the offer of money that stresses
what you think is your mastery,
your marriage with royalty.
But I am grateful for your coming.
It will comfort me to speak of your betrayal
and it will hurt you more to hear it.

I won the Golden Fleece
for you. Then, forsaking my home
and my loved ones, I followed you,
deepening in love, diminishing in wisdom.
Every danger you faced, I met and overcame.
I was your fighting spirit,
I was your sword,
but *you* accepted the glory.

And now, though I
have borne you children, you,
snake among men, have betrayed me
and arranged a new marriage.
Again I say I have borne you children.
If we had no children, I could
have understood why you decided
to marry again. A fresh love
for a new wife – this I
could have grasped. But what of
the pledges we made to each other?

You perplex my heart and mind.
Do you believe that the gods
of the old moralities are dead?
Do you believe that men and women
are now living under a new heartless, mindless morality?
Unhappiness is the wilful forsaking of the proven ways.
An oath is an oath.
Break an oath and the agile demons
of unhappiness leap through your
eyes and mind
and consume your soul.

Demons quarrel and bicker about the tasteful quality
of the soul. Some are bloated,
some shrivel and pine. Some die.
A dying demon is a piteous sight.
(*Pause.*)
A lost woman is a problem.
Jason, answer me this.
Where am I to turn?
Shall I go back to my father?

I betrayed my home and country.
I have nowhere to go.
I have made enemies everywhere
to add to your glory.
A woman kills or charms
that a man thrive and prosper.
What a faithful husband I have in you!
To prove it, I must be driven into exile,
deprived of friends, alone with my two sons.
At the wedding-feast
where stories flow like wine,
don't forget to tell the story
of two children and
a woman who once saved
your life and who are now, all three,
wandering in sluggish beggary.
O gods, why have you
taught us to distinguish gold
from tinsel, yet never
told us how to look at
men's thick bodies so that we
may tell the decent from
the rotten heart?

CHORUS. What does Jason know of Medea's rage?

JASON. It seems I need some skill in speech
to escape the roaring storm of your words.
You have told me what you think.
Let me tell you what *I* think.
It was the Goddess of Love herself
who saved me from the dangers of my quest.
You are a woman gifted
with eloquence and wit

and yet you're but an instrument
in the hands of the Goddess of Love.
It was the Goddess who enabled you
to save my life. Yes, you helped me,
but as I shall now demonstrate to you,
in logical fashion,
you gained much more than you lost.

First you quit a savage land
to live in this dear place where you have come to know
the subtleties of Law and Justice,
rather than the crude ignorance of strength.
Here, men appreciate your wisdom,
you have grown famous in their hearts and minds.
If you were living on some remote island
nobody of consequence would know your name.
May I never have a mite of gold in my house,
may I be denied the gift to sing
a sweeter song than Orpheus,
if my good fortune is to be hidden from men's eyes.
Men have the right to see
and to rejoice in what I've done.
They have the right to know the famous name of Jason.
That is all I have to say
about my finding of the Golden Fleece.
(After all, it was you who started this debate.)
(*Pause.*)
Next, there is the matter of
my marriage with the Princess.
What sane man is not attracted to royal blood?
In this particular matter, which I
consider wise, inevitable and just,
I shall demonstrate three indisputable things:
first, my instinctive wisdom;
second, the sanity and rightness of my choice;
third, the noble service I have
rendered to you and to my sons.
(Please, please hold your tongue
a moment. Have the courtesy
to give me time to speak.)
(*Pause.*)
When I came to this land,
a total stranger in an alien culture,

carrying on my back a load of troubles
my mind festering with painful problems,
what better luck or sweet good fortune
could I, a miserable exile, have
than marry with the King's daughter?
It was not that I was weary of your beauty
(that is the thought that cuts you to the quick
and puts the lightening-madness in your eyes)
or that I was crazy with desire for a young wife;
still less that I wanted to be the father
of many children. The children I have
are enough for me, I have no complaint
or criticism to make of them. No!
what I desired was a comfortable home
where we would always have enough
(for I know well a poor man has no friends
while money binds us together in firm friendship);
and so I wanted to see my children reared
in a manner worthy of their father
and his house. I wanted with all my heart
to give them a proper style
and, fathering other children
to be brothers to the children of your womb,
bring them all together
under one harmonious roof
in health and wealth and happiness.
It was a dream, Medea,
my dream of happiness.

Why should you want more children?
As for myself, it will reward me
to help the children I already have
by means of the children of my new marriage.
Surely that is no evil scheme?
I know you would agree
if jealousy were not binding you.
Why are you so blind, Medea, so tragically blind?

I know that you
women believe that to be lucky
in love is to be lucky in
all things, but if some curse
or sad misfortune hits that love,

you will consider this reasonably decent world
a vile, detestable place.
The world does not change
because of one woman's change of heart.
The gods, in their divine imagination,
should have devised a different way
for men to gather children.
Why should men depend on women to give them children?
Women should not exist.
That way, there would be no trouble in the world.

CHORUS. Jason, you arrange your arguments with plausible skill.
And yet you have betrayed your wife.
There is no arguing with that.

MEDEA. Yes! I have many beliefs
that are not shared by many people.
I believe, for example, that
the plausible traitor is the worst kind of scoundrel.
Plausibility smothers the soul with oily words.
By comparison, a passionately meant
insult is a kind of compliment,
a sort of spiritual bomb to shatter lethargy.
The plausible man, confident in his
ability to convince you of his evil
with fine words symmetrically arranged,
shrinks from no evil persuasion, because
evil persuasion is his purpose and his mission.
And how elegantly he would accomplish it.
There are those who envy him his style.
I have noted that this city is replete
with such men of style, and furthermore,
and sadder still, young men who wish
to imitate the plausible, successful men.
Every plausible man is clever
but it is a limited cleverness.
One burning word of honesty
is enough to reveal its emptiness.
If you were a man,
I mean a man of ordinary honour,
you would have told me about your
intended marriage to the Princess,
not kept it a secret from your sons and me.

JASON. And if I'd told you, I'm sure
    you'd have been ablaze with enthusiasm.
    Even now, you can't conceal the hate
    and resentment in your eyes.

MEDEA. No, my plausible man. You
    knew I was ageing, and this
    would do nothing to advance your plans.
    I had outlived my usefulness.

JASON. I say again, it was not for the sake
    of a woman that I enter marriage.
    I wanted you to live here in safety.
    I wanted to father princes
    to be brothers to my sons.
    I wanted royalty to spread through my family.
    I wanted to distance myself
    from poverty and want and shame.
    I wanted to kill all possible indignity.
    I wanted to establish, forever, a noble family.
    Glory to heaven for such a family.

MEDEA. May that family never be mine.
    I want no happiness that hurts my soul.
    I want the happiness that comes
    from *my* husband and *my* children,
    mine alone.

JASON. Will you change your
    prayer to the gods, to find better
    sense in yourself? Say – 'May I
    never see a useful opportunity as being
    shameful; may I consider
    no good fortune as being ill.'
    The best prayer is the prayer
    that helps us to cope
    with the folly and evil of this world.
    Pray to make sense of the swirling world.

MEDEA. Your prayer for sense –
    the commonest of common sense –
    is an insult.
            Prayer is not
    a way of coping with fools.

Prayer is for dealing
with the injustice *caused* by fools,
rhetorical idiots
and blind, ambitious,
power-hungry cretins.
Prayer, my plausible friend, is
anger at what is, and a longing
for what should be.
Prayer is a bomb at the door of your house.
Being a man of sense,
you have a palace of refuge.
Living my passion,
I am faced with exile.

JASON. You make your own exile.

MEDEA. But what was my crime? Did I
betray you and marry another
man so that I could be
the mother of a Royal Family?

JASON. You cursed the King.
You heaped curses on the head
of the ruler of this land.
You met his hospitality
with your obscene ingratitude.

MEDEA. On you, and on your house,
I shall heap such curses
you'll wish you'd never lived.
The only blessing you will ever know
will be your death. That's the blessing
you will pray for.

JASON. Listen, woman, listen carefully.
I have no wish to continue this absurd conversation.
If you wish me to help you
and my children in your exile, please
mention it to me. I'm prepared
to give all the help I can
with all the generosity in my heart.
I'm prepared to send letters of introduction
to all my powerful foreign friends
who will see to it that you are treated well.

I have a certain influence
which I'm prepared to use on your behalf.
You will not regret it, I assure you.
If you reject this offer, woman,
you are both foolish and mad.

MEDEA. Your friends mean nothing to me.
I will not use those I do not know.
For the life of me, I cannot accept
anything from you.
Do not offer me anything of yours.
The gifts of men like are plagues.
They spread contagion among those who touch them.
You are the poison of my life, Jason, the poison of my life.

JASON. Again, I say again
that I am willing to help you
and my two sons in every way.
You do not know
what is good for you and for them.
Think of the children, woman.
Think of their future.
If you think of others
your anger will weaken, then disappear.
But you are obstinate,
hugging your anger to your breast
like a favourite child.
Your obstinacy and anger
will cut you off from all your friends.
You will suffer more and more.

MEDEA. Get out of my sight.
There's a young wife waiting for you.
Enjoy her.
One day, perhaps, you will beg
the gods to unmake what seems
the happiness of this fresh union.
So many happy, radiant ceremonies
end in evil.
So out of my sight, plausible man.
Enjoy your new wife, while you can.
(*Pause.*)

Exit JASON.

If the bad strain in a man's love
that once seemed wholesome and true
poisons a woman,
what is she to do?
Should she surrender to that poison,
allow it to spread through her days and nights
until she's dead and forgotten?
Should she pretend, as many women do who want a lover,
the poison does not exist, and so
let it spread, fester and grow
within her till it rots her soul
and all she can do is smile, smile
in poisoned helplessness
at her poisoner and his like?
Let other women live and die as they will,
conquer or surrender according to their style,
let their hearts be poisoned
till they stink of servile hell,
I will not be poisoned by Jason
or by any man.
My heart is strong with that conviction
and I will show it.
If there's poisoning to be done
I will do it.

The time has come
to turn Jason's world upside down
and inside out.
The time has come
for me to act my grief
and for Jason to discover
that in certain unsuspected ways
death may be a matter of relief
from a woman's annihilating pride
when she knows, at last, that she's been cast aside.
Thrown out like an old rag, I know what's true.
I have a single day to do what I must do.
I shall accomplish more in that one day
than Jason in his lifetime; Jason, home-loving Jason,
who told me how to pray.

PART ONE

CHORUS. Love knows no limits
and may involve man in dishonour,
shame, drugs, drunkenness, street-wandering,
confronting strangers, sleeping
in rainy doorways, even death.
But if the love is wisely, precisely
measured, there is no richer
blessing.

Therefore, I pray. O goddess, never let
mad passion consume my heart
but honour me with the gift
of moderation. Moderation is
heaven's fairest gift,
the very sanity of the gods, their
sense of fair play at its sweetest
and most honourable. Moderation keeps
the demons of excess at bay,
and makes us grateful for the gift
of limits.

To live within limits is to
honour the infinite, mysterious
potential of excess. To live by rule
is to respect every rule-breaking passion
of which the heart is capable.
No remorse, no recriminations, no
vicious, angry quarrels – but I want
no sluggishness, deadness or
lethargy either. I want moderation.
I want the lively consciousness
of denying myself. I'm not speaking of tameness
or timidity, I'm speaking of conscious
moderation.
                    O gods, never
may I be without my city.
I would rather die than be
without this city.
There is no sorrow like that
of shameful exile. You have
no friend to turn to in your sickness,
no affection in the eyes
of people in the streets.

111

May the gods
protect me from the man who
would drive me from my city
and its affections. I fear that man
because I love my home.
My truest home is moderation – it's
like living in a house of courage.

Enter AEGEUS, *in traveller's dress.*

AEGEUS. Medea, may the gods grant you
the best of health.

MEDEA.   And to you, Aegeus.
Where are you coming from?

AEGEUS. I've just left the ancient oracle of Phoebus.

MEDEA. Why did you go to the oracle?

AEGEUS. I wanted to know how I might get children.
I wanted to be a fertile man.

MEDEA. And at this stage of your life
are you still childless?

AEGEUS. It seems to be the gods' will that
I am still without a child.

MEDEA. Are you married?

AEGEUS. Yes. Every night we sleep together.

MEDEA. Tell me, Aegeus, what did Phoebus
have to say about children?

AEGEUS. His words were too strange and twisted for me
to understand.

MEDEA. May I ask the god's reply?

AEGEUS.   It takes
a cunning mind to grasp these words.

MEDEA. Tell me, then, what was the oracle?

AEGEUS. I was advised not to let my best wine flow until –

MEDEA. Until?

AEGEUS. Until I return in safety to my home.

MEDEA. Then why do you come here?

AEGEUS. There is a king, the King of Troezen...

MEDEA. A holy man.

AEGEUS. To him, I will reveal the oracle of the god.

MEDEA. He knows a great deal about such matters.

AEGEUS. Yes, and of all the men at whose side
I fought, he is the one I loved most.

MEDEA. I wish you the best of luck, and may
you gain what your heart desires.

AEGEUS. Medea, why are your eyes so sad?
Where is the true beauty of your face?

MEDEA. Jason is wronging me. I never wronged him.

AEGEUS. What has Jason done? Speak plainly.

MEDEA. He has another wife who shares his bed
and shows her power over me, the mother
of his sons.

AEGEUS. Has he done such a shameful, such
a tormenting thing?

MEDEA.   He loved me once.
Now he casts me aside.

AEGEUS. Is he in love? Does he hate your touches?

MEDEA. Yes, this is his grand passion. Nothing else
matters to him.

AEGEUS. Forget him, then, since he has betrayed
his wife and children.

MEDEA. He wants a king for a father-in-law.
He wants power, royalty, and young love in his bed.

AEGEUS. Who gave him the bride?

MEDEA. Creon, the ruler of this country.
(*Pause.*)
My life is in shreds.
(*Pause.*)
Creon is driving me into exile.

AEGEUS. How does Jason allow this?

MEDEA.   I beg of you,
    Aegeus, to show pity for my misery.
    Do not stand apart and see me
    driven, helpless and alone, into exile.
    Receive me as a guest into
    your own country.

    I shall pray the gods
    to send you the children that
    your heart desires.

    The path you took to me
    was a path of pure good luck.
    I shall end your state
    of childlessness. I shall help you
    create wholesome heirs of your blood.

AEGEUS. With that promise, you have rescued me from madness.
    But let me tell you exactly where I stand.
    If you yourself come to Athens, I shall
    protect you in every possible way.
    But I must give you this warning: I shall
    not agree to take you with me out of this
    city of Corinth. If you yourself come
    to my palace, you will find a perfect
    refuge and a home. I shall
    never surrender you to any man.
    But you must escape from this city
    through your own efforts.
    I'll not be accused
    of treachery by my host.

MEDEA. You will not be accused of treachery.
    Let me have your oath.

AEGEUS. Do you not trust me?

MEDEA. Yes. I trust you. But in this city
    I have powerful enemies, eager
    to destroy me. If you were bound
    by oath, you would never hand me
    over to my enemies, if they tried
    to extradite me. But a friendly
    agreement of mere words, unstrengthened

by any sacred written pledge,
could easily be melted by shrewd
diplomatic tongues that could persuade you
to become their friend. I have
no power, whereas my enemies
live in the splendour
and power of palaces. That is why
I need your oath.

AEGEUS. You are wise, you are foreseeing.
I will do your bidding.
Dictate the oath.

MEDEA. Swear by the Earth, the Sun
my father's father, by all
the gods, by all –

AEGEUS.   To do what?

MEDEA. Never to expel me from your country,
and never to surrender me
willingly, to any of my enemies.

AEGEUS. I swear by the Earth, by the sacred
splendour of the Sun, by the entire
family of gods, to be true
to the oath that you propose.

MEDEA. And if you break that oath,
what punishment do you pray
to receive?

AEGEUS. The eternal doom of sacrilegious men.

MEDEA. I shall come to your city when I have done
what I intend to do.

Good luck and joy be with you on your journey.

CHORUS (*As* AEGEUS *departs.*)
May the Protector of travellers bring you safe.
May you be the father
of gifted and beautiful children.

MEDEA. O God of justice, magnanimous light of the Sun!
The time has come, my friends, my sisters,
when I shall sing victory-songs
over the bodies of my enemies.

Now I know my enemies will pay the penalty.
Just when all my plans seemed lost and scattered,
Aegeus appeared from another country where,
my work being done, I can live in safety.

Now, my sisters and my friends, let me tell you of my plans.
I shall ask Jason, through a servant, to visit me.
When he comes, he will find every word of mine submissive.
I shall tell him, with all the sincerity
at my command, that I am happy at his royal marriage,
that I have decided it is the best of all good things.
I shall ask him only to permit my children to stay here.
Not that I shall leave them in a land,
a bristling hostile place, for my enemies to insult.
I shall send my sons with gifts for the bride
that she may feel disposed to leave my children in this place.
A handsome robe and a head-dress of beaten gold.
If she puts on the robe, she will die in agony.
Not only she, but anyone who touches her.
Such is the invisible poison in which I steep my gifts.
What I must do next fills me with horror.

I must murder my two sons.
(*Pause.*)
When I have destroyed the house
of Jason, poisoned his princess
and murdered my sons, I'll quit
this land of curses.
No man alive will take my sons from me.
The safety of the grave is preferable
to the sneers, jeers, contempt and mockery
of this world.
My sons will be safe,
without father, without home, without refuge from danger.
And now, I admit my life's great error.
I left my father's house, seduced
by Jason's oily words. But heaven is
my friend, and Jason shall pay for his crime.
He'll never see his sons again in this life.
He'll never father a child from his fresh young
princess. She will die the death she deserves,
the death of my poison. Nobody
on this earth will call me weak.

Medea is the real strength
of woman, the strength that
for centuries has been subdued,
submerged and piously enslaved.
No, I am not weak.

I am a devoted friend,
a deadly enemy.
In its heart of hearts,
that is the kind of person
the world most admires.
I am set to win the admiration of the world –
for what it's worth!

CHORUS. I beg you not
　　to commit these murders.

MEDEA. There is no other way for justice to be done.
　　Murder is the instrument of justice.
　　You have not suffered wrong like me.

CHORUS. It would be like cutting the heart
　　out of your own breast.

MEDEA. I will murder my sons.
　　That is how I can hurt my husband most.
　　Hurting my husband is the purpose of my life.
　　No hurt, human or inhuman, can hurt him enough.

CHORUS. This will make you the most miserable
　　woman in the world.

MEDEA. Let it. From now on, words are
　　useless. (*To the* NURSE.) Please
　　go now and courteously request
　　Jason to visit me. Whenever I
　　need loyalty, it is to you
　　I turn. Say nothing of what
　　I intend to do; you are
　　a woman and my loyal servant.
　　Stay true to me: bring Jason here.

Exit NURSE.

CHORUS. Medea, do not murder your children.
　　You murder your own flesh and blood
　　but plan your own safety

117

in one of the most fragrant and fertile
countries under the Sun, favoured by
heaven from the beginning. These people
are children of the blessèd gods.
Love lives in the air.
                            Will you dare,
killer of your own children, to enter
and live in that land of sacred rivers
and hospitable homes? It is sacrilege
that you should even think of living there.
Think, Medea. Think of the nature
of sacrilege. Think, o think, Medea.
You are stabbing your children.
They are on their knees, they cry for mercy.
'Mother! Mother! Do not murder us.'
Think, Medea, think. You will be,
forever, Medea the murderess
of her own children. It would
have been more merciful
to kill them in the womb.
Abortion can be a kind of mercy.
But to let them look into the eyes
of people, to let them see the miracle
of the changing of the seasons,
to let them watch the birth and growth
and death of flowers, to let them
walk through gardens, to feel
the blessing of the summer rain,
the rebel outburst of Nature in the Spring,
the way people are born and live and die,
to learn to speak, to listen to
the fluent miracle of words – that is
a crime as great as the crime
of killing them now.
Where in the hardness of your heart
did you think of such a plan?
And in that horrible moment
when you kill your own children
where will you find the steel
to make inhuman your heart and hand?
When you look into their eyes,
Will you not go out of your mind
to know you are their murderess?

When your two sons fall at your feet
begging for mercy,
will you not go mad
when their innocent blood
stains your hands?
You bore them gladly in your womb.
Will you send them in great agony to their graves?
My heart will not believe it.
Your heart will never bear it.
You are not exacting revenge.
You are embracing madness.

Enter JASON.

JASON. What are you looking for, woman?

MEDEA. Jason, I ask forgiveness for everything I said.
  After all the love you gave me, I can rely
  on you to put up with my tantrums
  and my fits of temper. I've been thinking
  the whole situation out for myself.
  Bitter bitch (that's how I saw myself),
  what madness of mind and heart makes me
  hate those who wish me nothing but good?
  What madness made me treat as enemies
  the just and royal rulers of this land,
  and my husband who, in taking a princess
  for a wife, ensuring brothers for his sons,
  is merely doing what will benefit us all?
  What is wrong with me? Why am I still
  enraged when the gods pour
  blessings on my head? Do I not have
  gifted children of my own? Has it slipped
  my mind that I am an exile
  from my own land, lacking
  real friends? These thoughts have
  shown me how foolish I have been,
  how blind to your generosity,
  how selfish towards your selflessness
  and how pointless are my jealousy and hate.
  Now, dear Jason, I wish to thank you.
  You are doing the right thing in choosing
  this beautiful young wife.

I have been the greatest fool in the world.
I should have encouraged your plans,
helped you to fulfil them,
even stood by the marriage bed
and helped, as best I could, the young bride.
But I am what I am...a woman,
a mere woman. I beg forgiveness,
and admit my hideous mistakes.

But now, I have turned
my mind towards sanity and hope
and sincere co-operation. I have but
one desire – to help you build your happiness.
Your happiness is mine, as my heart is always yours.

Children, children, please
come here, please leave the house,
come out and greet your loving father
as I have done. Speak freely with
your father. Stand with
your mother in binding us all
together in family love, forgetting
all that former hate. The nightmare
is over; the light of love shines
through again. Take your father's
right hand.
          O God, what strange
sickness attacks my imagination?
My children, will you stretch out
your arms like that in eternity?
My tears are quicker now than
they have ever been. My fears
are bursting my heart, freezing
my blood. It is those sleepless
nights of rage and hate that
blind my loving eyes with tears.

CHORUS. I cry as bitterly as you. I cry
    because of the sheer waste that hate creates.
    I pray that hatred vanish from the earth.
    It does more harm than racking famine.

JASON. That's the kind of talk I like to hear, woman.
    I can forgive what happened in the past.

it's natural enough for women to resent
men who marry other women,
especially younger women.
Women hate ageing, it makes their skin
like dry, wrinkled seaweed.
The sea rejects it and the land withers it.
It is sad and feeble to the touch.
It has no heart to live in its true element.
But you have changed your heart,
Medea, and for the better. It took
quite a while, of course, but at last
you have seen the happy light of reason.
From being a woman of vile abuse
you have become a wise woman.
And as for you, my sons, I have not
forgotten you. You are now perfectly safe.
I know that you will occupy
the most important positions
here in the city, with your brothers.
All you have to do now is grow to be men
like me, like Creon, like the great men of the city.
Your father, and his strong friends,
will see to the rest. May I see you,
rock-like and determined, in the full bloom
of your youth, annihilate my enemies.
Medea, why are you crying?

MEDEA. The children. I was just thinking about
the children. Growing up…becoming
men…

JASON. Why are you crying about the
children? There's no need for it.

MEDEA. I am their mother. A few moments
ago, when you were talking about
long life, grief swept through me,
because I thought their lives might
not turn out as brightly as you
predicted. I was briefly
haunted by the possibility of some
tragic disappointment, some knife
or poison in the heart of hope.

JASON. Be cheerful, Medea, I'll see to it
that things turn out for the best.
All we need is courage and determination.
Time, and the will to be important in this world,
will take care of the rest.

MEDEA. We women are weak creatures.
It takes very little to make us cry.

Just one thing remains to be said.
Since I must go into exile
(and now I see that is a just decision)
I pray that out two sons
are reared by your kind, commanding hand.
Please ask Creon to let
the children stay.

JASON. I shall ask him.

MEDEA. You could ask your wife
to intercede with Creon,
to let the children stay.

JASON. Creon will grant
permission, if I can
persuade my wife.

MEDEA. In this respect, I'd like to play my part.
I want to send the children with gifts to her,
gifts far more beautiful than any gifts
men make in these modern times:
a noble robe, and a head-dress of beaten gold.
Let there be no delay. Let one of my maids
bring the gifts immediately. What joy,
what boundless joy, will come into the heart
of your young bride, to have not only
a husband of your heroic stature,
but also finery which the Sun of all
the Heavens, the light of all the earth,
my own father's father, gave to his children.

MEDEA *takes the casket from the* NURSE *who has brought it and gives
it to the* CHILDREN.

Dear children, take these wedding gifts
to the Princess, the happy bride,
and give them to her

with all your natural grace.
These incomparable gifts will mean
something very special to her:
incomparable gifts best suit an incomparable woman.

JASON. Medea, you are as obstinate a woman now
as when we lived together.
Why do you give your richest gifts away?
Do you think a palace such as mine
is short of finery and gold?
Hold on to these gifts, keep them, you'll need them yet,
do not give them away. If my wife respects me,
she will prefer me to all the wealth in the world
I'm sure of that. Can't you see
my wife will not be swayed by gifts:
she will be swayed by me.

MEDEA. Please, please permit me to give your wife these gifts.
Gifts please even the gods, and gold
is mightier than a million words.
In you, she has the greatest fortune of our time.
Her existence makes the gods excited.
Heaven trembles with admiration at this woman on earth.
She is young, her father is a king.
To save my children from exile,
I would surrender my life,
not merely give my gold.

So go, my children,
go to the palace and ask your father's
beautiful young wife to let you stay in this city.
(*Pause.*)
Place the crown in her delicate hands.
It is most important that you do exactly that.
She must take my gifts into her own hands.
Go as quickly as you can, there is no time
to lose. May the gods attend
your every step, and may you bring back
news to make your mother's heart
as happy as she could dream it to be.

Exeunt CHILDREN, TEACHER, JASON *and* NURSE.

CHORUS. Now, all the hope I had is dead.
The children are in their graves already.

The bride will wear her priceless head-dress.
Death will come to her in a circlet of gold.
Her own hands will accomplish this,
standing in front of a mirror.
How gracefully she'll step into the dress of death.
Splendid robe, circlet of beaten gold –
wedding gifts beyond her royal dreams.

Poor girl! Poor bride! Poor, poor Princess!

And you, poor, cocky Jason – unwitting
bringer of death to your own children.
Where is your royal family now?
Where is your man's dream of happiness?
Poor man. Poor Jason. Poor, poor seeker.
And now, Medea, I cry for you.
You will kill because you were betrayed.
That is the one terrible fact
that consumes your heart and mind,
and makes your life a sword
to be plunged into Jason's heart,
a plausible man in a royal bed.
I see all things clearly now
and all the hope I had is dead.

Enter CHILDREN *with their* TEACHER.

TEACHER. My lady, here are your two sons,
    saved from exile. The royal bride
    graciously and gladly accepted your gifts.
    She took the gifts into her delicate, royal hands.
    Your sons have made glad, smiling peace with her.
    But what is wrong? What is the matter?
    Why are you so upset, when fortune
    smiles on you?
    Why do you turn away your face?

MEDEA. Misery of hell!

TEACHER. These words have nothing to do
    with the happy words I have brought to you.

MEDEA. Misery! Misery of hell!

TEACHER. Have I made a mistake?
    Have I unwittingly said evil words?
    I thought my words were good.

Where have my words gone wrong?
What is my mistake?

MEDEA. Your words were...your words.
I do not blame you for your words.

TEACHER. Why are you crying

MEDEA. Because I must, old man, because I must.
The gods had a hand in this
My folly played its part as well.

TEACHER. Be hopeful, Medea. One day, your
children will bring you to your home.

MEDEA. Long before that day, I shall
bring them and others
to a different home. There are countless
kinds of home in this homeless world.

TEACHER. Many women have been
separated from their children.
We're only human and must put up
with all these troubles as patiently as we can.

MEDEA. I shall do precisely that.
I shall endure whatever happens.
Now please go inside
and prepare the usual food
for my children.

Exit TEACHER.

My children, o my children. A city is
assured for you where you will live
without me. But I face exile
in an unknown land, before I have set eyes
on your happiness, before I have
seen your brides, prepared your
marriage beds, and held high
the burning torches of good will.

My own self-will has
brought me to my misery. My sons,
did I rear you all for nothing?
Was it for nothing that I bore
the agony of your birth? There was a time
when I hoped you'd be near me

125

in my old age, and with your loving hands
prepare my body for the grave.
That dream is dead. Without you,
my children, mine will be a life of pain,
while you, in another land, will
never see your mother with your tender eyes.
                              Why do
your eyes look into mine? Why smile
into my soul with your final smile?
What am I to do? Women, my heart
is water at the sight of my children's faces,
descended from the Sun. I cannot do it.
Goodbye to all the schemes and plans I had.
I shall take my children with me
into exile. Why should I hurt or
madden their father by *their* misfortune,
only to double my own grief?
No, I will not do it.
I shall bury my plans, not my children.

What is this? What is wrong? What has softened me?
I will not make a fool of myself
by letting my enemies strut about in
freedom? I *will* do it. I *will* go
through with it.

Come, my children.
Go into the palace.

The CHILDREN *move towards the door of the palace, stand there as*
MEDEA *speaks to the* CHORUS.

Whoever here doesn't
wish to witness my sacrifice
may simply turn away. My hand
is as determined as my heart.

My heart! Do not commit
this crime. Leave them alone,
leave them the right to live their lives
as they will. Even if they live
in a far country, the knowledge
that they are alive will bring me
joy enough. Knowledge that those

we love are alive and well brings
a special joy to the thinking heart.
No! No! By the dead in hell who
are condemned never to forget their crime,
this love cannot be. No son of mine
will take an insult from an enemy.
My sons must die.
I, who gave them birth, will kill them.
That woman will not escape.
Already, she wears the golden diadem
of poison on her head.
And in the poisoned robe
the shining bride is dying.
I have knowledge
of such matters – there are consequences.
Jason's beautiful young princess is dying at this moment.
I wish to speak to my children.
Let me hold your hands,
my sons, let me kiss your hands.

O dear hands of my sons
O dear mouths of my sons
O dear dear figures of my dreams
O open and noble faces
may you be happy forever
but not here.
Your father has stolen your happiness from you.
How sweet it is to touch you,
how soft is your skin,
how sweet is your breath,
my children, children of my womb.
Go! Go now! I cannot bear to look on you.

The CHILDREN *go inside.*

Grief and misery are my masters now.
Passion strangles all my love,
passion brings most of his unhappiness to man,
passion that gives fierce strength to my will.
It is my own loved children I must kill.

CHORUS. The fathers of children
are not as happy as the men
who have no children.

127

A man without children
never knows if children
are a blessing or a curse
and so he cannot miss a happiness
he never had, and therefore may
escape a life of slavish misery.
But those whose homes are full
of growing children that they love
are often eaten by anxiety and worry,
day after day, night after night.
How are they to rear them properly?
What schools shall they send them to?
How shall they speak to them?
How show authority and not appear tyrannical?
How be patient in the face of disobedience?
How reprimand a child without alienating him further?
And then, if educated, how shall children make a living?
If uneducated, what can be done for them?
How tolerate their surly silences,
their foolish babble, their
unbelievable friends with clowns' faces
and hair like the plucked feathers
of a thousand different birds?
How tolerate the garish absurdity
of growing up? And finally,
suppose the children have grown up properly,
how can the father know
if the child is good or bad,
ready to help the father in his old age
or ditch him like a toothless old dog?
Many a father knows what it means
to be driven into exile
in the land that helped him rear his family.
I know many a father in this city,
not far from where his son begets
more sons. It is ludicrous succession.
Many women are aware of this,
but keep their silence. What is the use of talking?

Enter MESSENGER.

MEDEA. It's curious
how evil makes men hurry,
shakes them from their lethargy.

MESSENGER. Go, Medea, get out of here.
Get out, by land or sea.
Get out! Get out!

MEDEA. Why?

MESSENGER. The Princess is dead.
So is her father, Creon.
Both dead by your poison, planted
in your beautiful gifts. Your gift
of poison has brought death and havoc.

MEDEA. From this moment, you are my friend and ally.
Already, I begin to know some peace of mind.

MESSENGER. Are you human? Do you know
what you have done?

MEDEA. Did she die in agony?

MESSENGER. When your children arrived with their father
at the palace, we rejoiced because we thought
your marriage troubles were over.
The servants whispered that you'd settled
your long quarrel with Jason. One servant
kissed your children's hands, another kissed
their hair. I myself, in joy, went
with the children to the women's rooms.
The Princess, who now occupies your place,
did not see the boys at first, but looked
at Jason longingly. Then, however,
resenting the children's presence, she
veiled her eyes and turned away her face.

Jason tried to calm her anger,
saying: 'Do not hate your friends.
Calm your temper and turn your
head this way. You must accept
your husband's friends as your own.
Please accept these gifts, and ask your father
not to send these boys into exile,
for my sake, for your strong husband's sake.'

Well, when she saw the gifts,
she relented, she promised all things
to her husband; and scarcely had Jason

and your sons left her
than she put on that most beautiful robe.
Carefully she placed the circlet of beaten gold
on her rich clustering hair
and began to achieve her perfection
before a mirror, smiling at her body.
Then she rose and walked across the room
on delicate white feet, so happy with her gifts.
Again and again, standing tall and stately,
she glanced at the dress falling in rustling beauty
round her feet.

There followed the most horrible sight
I have ever seen. The Princess's complexion
changed, she staggered to and fro,
she tried desperately to run, her limbs
were trembling like leaves
when the year is failing, and finally
managed to sink into her chair.
One of the oldest and most perceptive
of her attendants, believing she'd
been stricken by a fit of panic,
or some attack inspired by divine anger,
cried out her prayers to the gods
until she saw white foam furious on
her lips, the pupils of her eyes rolled up,
and every drop of blood abandoning her skin.
Immediately, a maid rushed out to Creon's palace,
another ran to Jason, to tell
the terrible news.
The house became a house of chaos.

Then the Princess, lying there, eyes closed,
groaned in agony, began to revive.
A double misfortune hit her then.
From the circlet of beaten gold upon her head
there flowed a pure consuming fire
while the incomparably beautiful robes,
the gifts of your innocent children,
began, with slow, efficient savagery,
to eat the Princess's immaculate white flesh.
Her body became a flame,
she leaped from her chair

and ran, shaking her head and hair
every way she could,
trying to throw the golden crown
off her burning head and hair.
But that circlet of beaten gold gripped hard.
Her most glorious hair became an insatiable fire
and the more desperately she shook her hair
the more fiercely the fire continued to burn.
Shrivelled and contorted by the agony of fire
she fell on the floor, and only her father
was able to recognise her, so charred
and melted her beautiful features.
Nobody could tell where her eyes were,
nobody discern the least sign of the beauty of her face.
She was a melting, ugly, burning thing.
The blood, mingling with fire, fell
in blazing drops from her head,
the flawless white flesh melted from her bones,
as the unseen poison consumed her, bit by bit.
This was the most fearsome thing I ever saw.
We were all afraid to touch the corpse,
appalled by poison and by fire,
by the black ruin that was once a fair princess.

But her father, ignorant
of what had happened, rushed into
the room and embraced the body.
Weeping and moaning, he kissed
his daughter's burnt form and cried:
'My child, my daughter, my poor daughter,
what god has brought this hideous
destruction on you?
Who burned the life out of
my only child?
O my daughter, let me be with you in death!'

When he had stopped crying and moaning,
he tried to stand upright
but he stuck to the dress
like ivy to the trunk of a tree
or an old wall. The struggles
of the old man were horrible to see,
so desperate, pathetic, futile, self-destroying.

Trying to free a leg, his daughter's
burnt body would stick to his,
and if he jerked violently, he ripped
his shrivelled flesh off his own bones.
At last, mercifully, he died.
Side by side they lay,
father and daughter,
King and Princess, unfleshed,
dead. Burnt bones.
Dead, Medea, dead.

There is no need for me
to speak of what's in store for you.
You know with what horrific precision
the punishment fits the crime.

The life of man is a shadow.
Those who are called philosophers
and masters of subtle reason
are most worthy of condemnation.
No living man knows lasting happiness
or even, perhaps, the meaning of it.
It is a pleasant word, though much
abused, and certainly misunderstood.
Two burnt corpses on a royal floor.
when good fortune flows this way or that
one man may have more money than another.
But happiness – I have no answer to that.

Exit MESSENGER.

CHORUS. Jason has been punished for his sin.
    Innocent princess,
    Jason's love is the cause of your death.

MEDEA. My friends, my sisters, mothers, wives,
    I am ready to kill my children
    and leave this land.
    I cannot delay, or my children
    will fall into murderous hands.
    Whichever way the wheel turns, my children must
    die. And if they must, *I* will kill them,
    I who gave them birth.
    Here is the sword.
    I must do it now.

No thinking of my children,
I have my unlived years to grieve for them,
yes, to grieve.
Though I shall kill them, at least I loved them.

CHORUS. O Earth and Sun, consider this accursed woman,
stop her before she murders her children.
Stop Medea from killing the children of light.
Protect the house from murder, and the curse
of the dead who don't forget.
For you, Medea, the pains of birth meant nothing.
Nothing do these lovely boys mean to you, Medea.
Why let anger poison your heart?
How can murder so easily take the place of love?
Women who dare to love, what sort of evil
do you create in men? What sort of evil
do you discover in yourselves? This thing called love,
how much of the world's evil has it created?

The CHILDREN *are heard within.*

The cries. The cries. Listen to the cries.

Enter JASON.

JASON. You there, standing in front of this house,
is Medea still inside? Or has she
escaped? She had better hide in the earth
or fly into the sky, if she wishes
to avoid my vengeance.

CHORUS. Jason, your children are dead,
murdered by their mother.

JASON. What?

CHORUS. Your children are dead,
murdered by their mother,
go see the corpses
in their blood.

JASON. The bodies. Let me see the bodies
(*Pause.*)
Where is that woman? Let me kill her!

MEDEA *appears in a chariot. She has the bodies of the* CHILDREN.

133

MEDEA. What's all this talk of killing?
   Are you searching for the bodies and me
   who did the deed? Don't bother. If you
   have something to say to me, say it now,
   but you shall never touch me. I have
   a magic chariot, a pure, unpoisoned gift
   of the Sun, my father's father, to protect me
   against my enemies, plausible man.

JASON. You are the coldest murderess that ever lived.
   You are an evil plague that will infect the world.
   There's a demon in you, whom the gods
   have set against me. You murdered your brother.
   Then you married me with your murderous
   heart. You bore my children whom you have
   murdered because I left your bed. You
   are not a woman, you are the embodiment of hate.
   May the devil take you for his wife,
   murderess of your children, and may you populate hell
   with monsters like yourself. I shall never
   see alive the children I begot and reared and lost.

MEDEA. You are a fool,
   as King Creon was a fool to grant me one day of freedom.
   You could not hope, nor could your princess hope
   to scorn my love, the love of magical Medea.
   You are a fool, thinking to make a fool of me,
   and live happily forever after, as in some childish legend.
   You and your princess and Creon are a legend of fools.
   Two fools burnt, the third fool
   a whimpering, abusive, shattered parody of man.
   Call me what you will, abominable, evil, poisonous.
   I don't care, now that I've got
   beneath your skin into your heart.
   That's the special poison
   I reserved for you.
   My grief is nothing when I know
   you cannot mock me. Your mockery is
   impotent as you will be. Sorrow,
   when deep enough, castrates a man.
   Do you not already feel a certain weakness,
   a certain helplessness? Will you be a father
   ever again? Give some thought to that.
   Ask yourself the simple question – what is Jason now?

JASON. I did not murder them.

MEDEA. You insulted me.

JASON. Because I scorned your love
you believed it was your right to murder?

MEDEA. You insulted me.

JASON. You are completely evil.

MEDEA. Your children are dead.

JASON. No! They live in me to bring
dread curses on your head.
(*Pause.*)
Let me bury my sons.

MEDEA. No! I shall bury my sons with my own hands,
taking them where no enemy may do violence
to their graves. In time, I shall,
through rites and rituals, expiate
their murder. I shall live with a man
of my choice. You shall die as you
deserve, now that you have seen
how death has so attended
your living marriage in a state
of gold and fire and agony.
Your promised blessing is your life's curse.

JASON. May the innocent blood of my children
drown you in endless nightmare.

MEDEA. Only a foolish God would listen to you,
breaker of oaths. And there are no foolish gods.
The world is full of foolish men.
Among such foolish men, you are the total fool.
(*Pause.*)
Go bury you wife.
You know little of grief now. Wait patiently
for your old age. Then, there's nothing
left but memory. Some griefs deepen
with memory, become more real
than when they happened first.
Do you look forward to old age?

JASON. O my children, o my dear, dear children.

MEDEA. Are you hurt, Jason? Jason, are you hurt to know
you're not the man who won the Golden Fleece
or planned a royal family
but a man, a poor, sad, pointless man
who has no wife, no home, no children?

JASON. My sons! My sons! Let me kiss their mouths.
For god's sake, let me touch the sweet, soft
skin of my children. Please, let me touch them.
Once, once only. Let me touch them once.

MEDEA. No, Jason. The truth is you gambled and lost.
You will never touch your children again.
I killed them. That is all you know.
I killed them. You will never touch them again.
That is all I permit you to know.
There's nothing left of you in me.
How much of me is left in you?

JASON. I curse you.

MEDEA. Curse yourself.
You never did; you never could
and that is why no god will
stoop to bless you.

Exit JASON.

CHORUS. Medea is in full possession of her own life
and of her beloved dead.
In a short time, Jason is a childless wreck.
The gods are not capricious, but they are
unpredictable. What was expected has not been
accomplished; what was unexpected has come
to happen. That is the end of the story.
And yet I wonder, and will always wonder –
Is Medea's crime Medea's glory?

EURIPIDES'
THE TROJAN WOMEN

A NEW VERSION

PREFACE

It's hard to say to what extent the writing of a certain kind of play leads one, directly or indirectly, to the writing of another. I felt, after I'd finished *Medea*, that I wanted to write another play about women. So many things had been left unsaid. They always are. Again I was drawn to Euripides, this time to *The Trojan Women*.

Almost fifty years ago, I heard women in the village where I grew up say of another woman, 'She's a Trojan woman, God bless her', meaning she had tremendous powers of endurance and survival, was determined to overcome different forms of disappoinment and distress, was dogged but never insensitive, obstinate but never black-scowling, and seemed eternally capable of renewing herself. And she did all this with a consciousness that seemed to deepen both her suffering and her strength. Over the years I've observed these qualities in various women in different towns, cities and countries.

So the word 'Trojan' travelled across Europe and across the centuries. In the much poorer Ireland of the 1940s and 50s, the word defined and dignified the hard-working lives of women whose husbands had gone to England to find work, to send money back home. Hecuba was Maggie, Mollie and Liz. And so, she is still remembered, and will be, when this *now* has become a new *then*.

Some scholars and critics refer to *The Trojan Women* as a passive play, more a stirring spectacle than a real drama. I re-wrote this version of Euripides' play many times; and as I re-wrote it I found that it became increasingly active, although the women's situation overwhelmingly said that they were passive victims at the whimsical mercy of their male conquerors. And yet, within that apparent passivity of victims, I increasingly found a strong, active, resolute and shrewd note. My problem was to convey this note of active resolution, so closely linked with seemingly utter hopelessness, in language that came in waves suggesting both the women's spirits and the sea itself. Again, as I re-wrote the play, the women became more and more real to me; it was this deepening sense of the reality of the various women that I found hardest to capture. A man is trapped in his own language. How could I find the words to let these women express the ever-deepening reality of their natures? Well, I tried.

I wasn't writing a hymn to heroic women although I believe a man might spend his lifetime praising certain women and count that life well spent. I tried to write an active drama exploring the complex reality of a few memorable women. It was their different kinds of intensity that I found most magnetic. This play tries to present those mesmeric intensities in a fit language.

BRENDAN KENNELLY
April 1993/2006

THE TROJAN WOMEN

Brendan Kennelly's *The Trojan Women* was first performed at the
the Peacock Theatre, the Abbey Theatre, Dublin, on 2 June 1993.
The cast at the first performance was as follows:

POSEIDON, *God of the Sea*	Birdy Sweeney
PALLAS ATHENA, *Goddess*	Helene Montague
TALTHYBIUS, *a Greek herald*	Martin Murphy
HECUBA, *widow of King Priam,*	
mother of Hector	Cathy White
CASSANDRA, *prophetess,*	
daughter of Hecuba	Fionnuala Murphy
ANDROMACHE, *widow of Hector*	Pauline McLynn
MENELAUS, *King of Sparta*	Sean Kearns
HELEN, *wife of Menelaus*	
(taken by Paris to Troy)	Ali White
CHORUS	Tina Kelleher
MUSICIAN	John Dunne
DIRECTOR	Lynn Parker
SET AND COSTUME DESIGN	Frank Conway
MUSIC DIRECTOR	John Dunne
STAGE DIRECTOR	Suzanne O'Halloran
ASSISTANT STAGE MANAGER	Micil Ryan

The play is set outside the ruins of Troy.

Battlefield after a battle. Walls of city at back, broken. Huts to right and left, at front, with chosen women to be taken away by the Greeks. HECUBA *is lying on the ground, asleep. Dusk of early dawn. The God* POSEIDON *dimly seen before the walls.*

POSEIDON. The war is over. When will another war begin?
    I'm a tired old god in an old, tired world.
    I've seen war piled on war, horror on horror, death on death.
    I've seen love too
    and I say this:
    Love will come to rule the world,
    that is, women will rule the world.
    Although what you're about to see
    might seem to say that women
    are the rags and tatters of humanity
    or, at best, the perks of war,
    women will rule the world.

    I know that. I know it in all my broken dreams.
    (Almost bemusedly.)
    Women will rule the world.

    When that day comes, I won't be as
    old and tired as I am now.
    Only good dreams can rejuvenate
    a weary god.

    I came up out of the sea.
    The cold, fearless freedom of the waves flows through me.
    I see people on the run from love,
    devoting themselves to slavery.
    They call it responsibility.
    Some people would make a slave of the sea,
    and poison it as they enslave it.

    I have good and bad dreams
    and I make things.
    I made that city.
    Look at it now! A ruin!
    Freedom laughed and prospered there.
    Then a horse, its belly packed with death,
    a big, lumpy, clumsy, magical horse
    nosed through the walls
    and captivated hearts
    with the ease of a child

getting its way with an old man
too tired or charmed to resist.
Men surrender in an evening
what they have spent their lives defending.
The city's freedom died in one fiery night.

Freedom is like health –
you never know it until you've lost it.

Look at that city – a ruin!
A dream of freedom in smithereens!
Limp and weary soldiers, dazed with victory,
wait for a wind to take them home
to wives and children left so long ago
they must be strangers now.

There's no stranger quite so strange
as the stranger waiting at home,
no stranger like the stranger in the bed.

Home? Home is often where strangers go to behave
as if they knew each other.
After war, strangers go home.

A war will make familiar love
into the strangest thing in the world.
War turns truth to lies and makes lies true.
I see my city –
scattered rags at my feet,
blackened bits of timber after fire, black as shame,
a bag of rubbish ripped asunder by starving dogs.
This is where good dreams grow feeble and sick.
Sick dreams spawn the evil of the world,
the river runs through the city's body like a shock.
The river is women's cries.
Women hover at the edge of war,
women are the spoils of war.
War breaks old ways,
creates new slaveries, new choices,
tramples old established laws to pieces
like children's bodies under the hooves of horses.
Women are spared the shedding of blood
to warm chosen beds.
Even now, victorious Greeks are drawing lots for women.
The war is over. It is time for prizes.

There are women hidden in these huts,
prisoners, slaves, prizes, warm melting fertile prizes.

Helen herself is a prize.
The most dangerously beautiful woman
in the world is a prize.
And Hecuba is a prize.
She lies here at the city's gates
crying of wrongs that can't be spoken.
Her face is brave, her tongue sharp, her heart broken.
But was there ever such a spirit in a woman's body?
Hecuba will fight to the end
and beyond the end.
Even in slavery, she struggles to be free.
But now, she is a prize.
Who will win her?
Hecuba's daughter, Polyxena, is a prize.
Grabbed from life, she will stare at a grave.
Imagine that! Staring, always staring, at a grave!
Cassandra is a prize, a virgin
chosen, favoured, impassioned by her god.
She must go to Agamemnon's bed.
The girl-virgin and the old gore-soaked killer king!
All the ravings in her heart
all the whirling pictures in her dreams
all the storm-thoughts in her head
all the sweetly crazed sensations in her body
are nothing now.
The virgin must lie down
with that old bagful of sin and sperm and war and death.
She must be the plaything of Agamemnon's lust.

Men kill each other
stab each other's hearts
split each other's heads
and then the damned survivors
take women to their beds.
Through the mucky fields of blood
an old man rucks in murderous havoc,
slaughtering everyone between him and his prize –
a virgin in his bed, her blood
the end of all, and the beginning.
The old style is with us still:
Kill and love! Love and kill!

He turns to go. PALLAS ATHENA, *goddess, becomes visible in the dusk.*

> And I, creator turned survivor, for I have learned
> to survive my own creations,
> must leave this city of my dreams,
> this old broken city
> that will always live in me.
> My heart is only
> smashed bits and pieces of my city.

PALLAS. Gentle Poseidon!

POSEIDON. Pallas Athena! Have you something to tell me?

PALLAS. I need a friend. Are you my friend?

POSEIDON. Do you pity
this old broken city?

PALLAS. Are you my friend?
Will you give me your helpful hand,
your strong mind?

POSEIDON. What have you to tell me?

PALLAS. I would give these Greek ships
a homecoming to remember.

POSEIDON. Your spirit is a knife.
The blade is hate and love and rage.
I see the knife in your eyes.

PALLAS. They wronged me
In my own holy place.
They have forgotten the obscenity
they committed against me.

POSEIDON. I know what Cassandra suffered
at the hands of Ajax. He dragged her off,
beat her, insulted her, ridiculed her body and mind.
How can a man who so humiliates a woman go unpunished?

PALLAS. Not a hand was laid on Ajax.
Not one Greek moved against him
as if the violence he'd inflicted on Cassandra
was nothing at all. These Greeks no longer
know the meaning of what they do.

POSEIDON. It was your hand
  gave Troy to the Greeks.

PALLAS. My hand is ready to strike them now.

POSEIDON. My heart is ready to help your hand.
  What's your desire?

PALLAS. A homecoming that means
  they will never reach home.

POSEIDON. Never, never reach home?
  You want to let them flounder forever?
  You want them to be
  lost and conscious forever in the sea
  wandering, wandering, never to come
  into the sanity of home? You want
  all these ships, packed with victorious men,
  to be lost, lost, never to be found again?

PALLAS. I want them to know that home
  is what is always in the mind and always out of reach.
  I want the sea
  to be a sea of death
  working for me.
  I want you to make the sea
  mad with its own ferocity,
  wild with the genius of its treachery
  till it grows thick and sluggish
  with lost Greeks.
  I want to see the day
  when Greeks will speak my name
  and know the meaning of the name they say.
  Poseidon, make the sea my friend.
  These Greeks have lost respect for me.
  Maybe they'll find it again
  at the bottom of the sea!

POSEIDON. I'll stir the sea to madness
  never known before
  until the bones of drowned men
  pile and thicken on the sea-floor.
  Bodies piled on bodies will litter every shore.
  Be on your way, your strength and pride
  deepen because heaven is on your side.

Your triumph-time will come
when the last ship leaves for home!

Exit PALLAS.

How stupid you are, how blind
all you who smash cities to the ground
violate the holy places
desecrate the graves of loved ones
and vilify the honoured dead.
All this you do, and more, and worse,
and never ask why.
Ask nothing, either, when it's your turn to die.

Slowly the day comes. HECUBA *wakes, looks about her.*

HECUBA. Lift my head! I will lift my head!

This is not the beautiful city I have known.
This is not the city whose every corner is part of me.
This is not my home.

I look, I look...I see...ruin, desolation, decay,
my children lost, my land trampled, my man cut down,
every shred of dignity a feather in the wind,
every decent heart turned into idiot, fool and muttering clown.

I watched over you, I watched...are you nothing at all?
Is my heart twisted? My mind strayed?
My words timid and weak?
Where can I turn for help?
Who will begin to listen to my voice
when it dares to speak
of pain in my bones, my flesh, my very blood?
In this morning-light, my body rocks with pain
caught in the rhythm of its cries,
my own tears burning music out of my eyes,
fierce cold burning music flowing far and wide
for what is lost, insulted, broken, ruined, dead.

Look at my city, look at my body,
this head, this neck, these hands, these lips, these eyes,
my city is lost, so is my country.
My body, heavy, waits, packed with the cries
of my dead husband, my dead children,
my dear dead friends.

146

My body waits – for what?
A man's eyes! A man's eyes will cover me,
examine me from head to foot.
A man's eyes
can look at me in public
as if I were his private property.
A man's eyes can say things to me
that his tongue would never dare to utter.
A man's eyes can be as bold
in the daylight streets of a city
as a knife in a killer's hand.
A man's eyes mock every rule and law
and scorn all decent boundaries.
A man's eyes can strip me naked in a way,
a lover's hands
would never know how to do.
A man's eyes can
rape me in the street
and not a single word need ever be said!
A man is going to look at me, his eyes will say –
I want you in my bed.
This man has killed other men,
this man is used to getting his way,
accustomed to winning:
winning is why he's alive.

He'll win me,
a prize, a trophy.
He'll wear me like a medal,
discard me like old skin.
Why not? The dead in the earth know
that such a man was born to win!

Yet, may not a woman
fight, yes, fight, here and now?
May not a woman
win?
How?

(She stares towards the Greek ships on the far shore.)

Ships! Ships!
Packed with merciless faces.
How did you find your way

into our holy places?
Over the waves you came
driven in savage joy
to mingle glory and shame
in the streets of Troy.

Ships! Why did you come?
For a woman? A woman:
the test of her maker's dream,
the test of all things human.
Havoc and death she brought
and ruin to me and mine
and she laughed in the eyes of men
as if her heart were divine.

As if her heart were divine!
And who am I...
Here at the door of a Greek king's house
with a heart that seems ready to die?
A woman without a home
riddled with grief for her dead
humiliation in her heart
confusion splitting her head.

(She gets up, calls to the other Trojan women in the huts.)

Women! Women! Come out! Come out!
It is time for you to make your cry.
Not the cry of men:
it is time for the cry of women now.
This is the cry that will deepen in time
never uttered till now, but uttered once
must be shrieked again and again.
This is the cry of a woman's soul
hitting the cities built by men
rocking the world from pole to pole.

A WOMAN *comes out from a hut. Others come out slowly, stealing out,*
afraid.

FIRST WOMAN. Why do you cry like that?
Deep in the hut
I heard your sorrow pouring out
in words that ripped and cut
their way into my fear.
Your sorrow and my fear

148

tell me that we
will never again be free.

HECUBA. The ships are moving on the shore.

SECOND WOMAN. The ships are coming alive.
The ships are packed with our people's gold.
The ships are waiting for us women.

THIRD WOMAN. What do the ships want?
What will the ships do?
Will they sweep us off as prisoners –
You, and you, and you?

HECUBA. I don't know. Contain yourself. You mustn't be
the victim of your fearful dreams.

FIRST WOMAN. We will be prisoners, slaves,
even now the grinning ships
prepare our doom.
They sail by their arrogant star
and mock at all we are.
Women, come out of your tents!
Come out and see the ships
that will take you to slavery.
COME OUT! COME OUT!

HECUBA. Do not wake Cassandra!
God has maddened her.
Conquering men will mock her.
Let me never witness that ridicule.
My city, O my city,
you are broken-lonely
and broken-lonely these men would have us go
to places we can't begin to know.
Do not wake Cassandra! She is driven out of herself
because God has breathed into her blood
something of his own sorrow at the devastation
caused by murderous men who want us now as prizes.

Other women come out.

FOURTH WOMAN. Dear Queen, I steal out of the tent
of the Greek King.
I steal, fearful and trembling.
You called. Why did you call?

149

Am I to die? Are we to die?
What is the meaning of your cry?

FIFTH WOMAN. The cries are coming from the ships,
the ships' cries must be heard,
every word a tyrant
on the lips of tyrants.

HECUBA. No. Look! It is the morning light,
strong, unstoppable and bright.
The day and all it brings of good and bad,
is yours and yours alone.
Women, although our hearts are grieving,
we are the light of morning.

FIFTH WOMAN. I am cold and weak with fear.

SIXTH WOMAN. Someone in the distance. A Greek!
A Greek is coming this way.

FIFTH WOMAN. Whose slave am I?
Who has won me as a prize?

HECUBA. Easy, easy! Keep your peace.
They're drawing lots for us.
Keep your peace.

FOURTH WOMAN. Where will they take me?
To some island without a name
where I must lie
under the sun and moon of shame?
Never, never again to see
my own city.
Where will they take me?
I stand here,
I wait for some man's finger
to point at me.
No need for him to say a word,
his finger will say it all –
I want you!
I WANT – YOU!

Who will look at me like that?

HECUBA. Where will I be taken?
Into some nightmare den
where I can never sleep, never awaken?

Into some house of drunken, mocking men?
Shall I become a battered slave,
used a moment, dumped again
like a withered flower on my own grave?
Or must I rear my enemy's children
to sneer and spit in my ageing face,
I who grew in love and joy
proud and happy in this place,
a Queen in Troy.

A WOMAN. (*To* ANOTHER.) What will you do?

THE OTHER. The ships will cry.
I will be dragged into a ship.
Shall I live or die?
I have my fingers, lips, face, eyes.
If I live, may I be wise,
wise enough to see myself
as men see me,
to use my eyes as I see them use theirs.
When someone looks at me and says
I want you,
may I be wise enough to make him think
he is a winner born.
We are losers now.
We know what winners want.
They will pass us from one to the other
like dishes at a feast.
We are bread and meat and fish and fruit and wine.
They will eat and drink, drink and eat
again and again.
We live to satisfy the winners.
How shall I satisfy my winner?
With all I have, my body,
I am nothing but my body,
my body, my only weapon.

ANOTHER. I have my child, I see my child,
he looks at me as though
he can't believe that I should ever go
away. Away. Is my child enslaved or free?
The ships are crying in the sea.

ANOTHER. A lost child! A crying sea!
  But there's worse, worse, waiting for me.
  A Greek's bed, a sneering Greek's bed.
  I would be free, free as the dead,
  free of a body digging my body,
  crying in the dark, lost and lonely,
  longing for my city where my dreams of love began.

ANOTHER. God's curse on every rutting man!

ANOTHER. To serve some idle bitch
  sprawled in the warm shade:
  'What kept you? Slave, be quick!
  Why have you delayed?
  Why do you shiver like a rat
  before boiling water scalds its throat?
  Fetch me a drink! Prepare my bed!
  My man wishes to rut.'

ANOTHER. Maybe I'll find a gentle place,
  A kind hand, a kind face...

ANOTHER. But not a scurrilous loud house
  where lewd voices bully us
  with vicious, stupid jokes
  and stupid, vicious words
  and horrid laughter raining down
  on our pain.

ANOTHER. Here comes a Greek from the ships;
  the usual arrogant air,
  triumphant set of the lips.
  What news does he bear
  for us who are slaves from now on?
  We are the booty of men,
  prizes the Greeks have won!

TALTHYBIUS, *with soldiers, enters.*

TALTHYBIUS. Hecuba, you know me: Talthybius.
  I bring news.

HECUBA. Women, you are looking at our fear.

TALTHYBIUS. The lots are cast, Hecuba, the lots are cast.
  Lives and loves are won and lost.

HECUBA. What man? What land? What heart? What head?
What hill? What glen? What house? What bed?

TALTHYBIUS. Each woman has her own road to travel,
her own cup to swallow,
her own bed to sleep in.

HECUBA. What is our fate?

TALTHYBIUS. You must ask about each woman in turn.

HECUBA. Cassandra?

TALTHYBIUS. She is Agamemnon's prize.

HECUBA. What?

TALTHYBIUS. Yes, Cassandra sleeps in the King's bed.
Her body burns and cools at his will.
It's her good fortune the King has favoured her.

HECUBA. Polyxena?

TALTHYBIUS. Your daughter?

HECUBA. Yes.

TALTHYBIUS. She must watch Achilles' tomb.

HECUBA. My daughter? To watch a tomb?
What can this mean?
What is the reason for this?

TALTHYBIUS. Your daughter's happy.
She has nothing to fear.

HECUBA. How is she? Where is she? What is she doing?

TALTHYBIUS. She watches Achilles' tomb.
That is all she does, all she must do.
One thing alone, one solitary duty
consumes the heart and mind of your Polyxena.
Your daughter's eyes must stare at the earth
where dead Achilles lies. That is all.
Staring at death is her life's work.

HECUBA. Andromache?

TALTHYBIUS. She belongs to Pyrrhus, Achilles' son.

HECUBA. How quickly women are lost
   when wars are won.

TALTHYBIUS. So much killing must bring some profit to someone.

HECUBA. (*Pause.*) Whose slave am I?
   To whom do I belong?

TALTHYBIUS. Odysseus, King of Ithaca.

HECUBA. Odysseus! Tricky, slithery Odysseus!
   A liar, sharp and pitiless,
   is Hecuba's master.
   Odysseus! No man on earth
   has such scorn for justice.
   Everything Odysseus says and does
   means one thing:
   every action, oath, right and wrong,
   even the hate of his lying tongue
   works to advance the tricky art
   of his false and twisted heart.
   Where men and women make love, Odysseus makes hate.
   He is the crookedest creature in the world.

   My master!

   Women of Troy, cry for me now.
   Cry for Hecuba this black hour.
   You may fare badly but at least
   you will not sleep with this beast.

FIRST WOMAN. Hecuba, you know your fate.
   But who is the new owner of my life?

TALTHYBIUS. Men, go fetch Cassandra. Bring her here
   As quickly as you can
   I will give her to the King
   And give these other women
   To the men who're waiting for them.
   What's that? What's that? There! There!
   What is that light? A fire!
   These women are setting fire to themselves!
   They're setting fire to their own bodies
   rather than go to our waiting ships.
   Quick! Quick! Bring the women out.
   If this fire puts women's bodies

beyond the pleasure-loving reach of men
the King's rage will burn my head.

HECUBA. There is no fire.
It is a body all alight with the breath of God.
It is Cassandra.

Enter CASSANDRA, *in white, a great torch in her hand, a garland on her head. She does not see othe others.*

CASSANDRA. I am going to be a bride. A bride!

Lift high the flame
I give this flame to God
I praise God's name
in field and sea and flower and cloud.

Lift high the flame
soon I shall be wed
a happy bride
blessed and loved in a king's bed.

Why are you crying?
A father dead? City on fire?
I go garlanded,
young bride of desire.

Lift high the flame
this torch is borne with pride
a girl sleeps her last sleep.
Enter a bride.

I offer fire to God
His fire lives in me
His fire fills a woman's love
with God's intensity.

I bid myself to live
as I have not lived before,
I bid myself to dance
over my father's bones.

Let me dance like sunlight now
where my dead father lies,
dance O my dancing feet
dance like the dancing skies

dance like the happy light,
let earth and heaven sing
here where I make this bright
and fiery ring.

(She makes a circle round her with the torch and visions appear to her.)

Is it you? How beautiful your face,
your eyes, your mouth, your brow.
Hear my prayer, please
be with me now.

Is it you? Am I still alone?
O laugh and dance with me.
Be the fire unknown to men.
Dance, dance eternally.

Come, praise the marriage-God,
greet him with songs of pride.
When the songs are scattered like dust,
still praise the bride.

Praise me, women, praise me now
and cry for the heart and head
of the man who must take me
into his bed.

FIRST WOMAN. She is out of herself.
　　Hold her, hold her tight, down,
　　or she'll run to the ships.

HECUBA. O my Cassandra,
　　woman, child, woman,
　　why do you ring yourself with savage fire
　　and speak wild words of impossible desire?
　　Your torch, your leaping, dancing torch
　　is far from the old dream of peace.
　　But this is what is.
　　You are the child and prize of war.
　　You know what the man said:
　　killing and death and howls of agony
　　are the pathway to our marriage-bed.
　　Give me that torch; it bears
　　nothing of the old, holy fire
　　and your frenzy will not restore it.
　　What can a woman learn from her grief?

156

If she is lucky, she will endure
and in enduring, pick up shreds of wisdom.
Women, take away this torch.
And now, on dear Cassandra turn your eyes.
Look at her. What is her fiery dance?
What is the music of her fiery cries?
(Taking the torch, she hands it to a woman.)

CASSANDRA. I will lie in Agamemnon's bed.
I will kill Agamemnon.
I will set his house on fire
as he set mine.
Out of his burning body
out of his burning house and bed
my father and my brothers
will come from the dead.
Whoever loves me against my will
teaches me how to kill!

(She checks herself. Then she goes deeper into herself.)

Let me go into my ecstasy.
Do not hold me from my ecstasy.
I must go down, down
into the pit, beyond the pit
of human darkness
to find my special light.
I will find my special light.

I will go down, down
beyond the dreams of murderers
beyond the murderer's blood on the black axe
beyond the black axe sunk in the bottomless swamp
beyond the thoughts of horror that are half-stopped by fear
beyond the girl raped in the whimpering laneway –
I will go down through that appalling night
to find my special light.

Already, I know something.

You and I and these women
are happier than the Greeks, our conquerors.
The power of God is in me.
Do not hold me from my ecstasy.
Let me tell you this.

One woman's beauty is the death of countless Greeks.
And what is the achievement of their King?
He killed love that hate might live.
He will die from dead love and living hate,
a conquering, strong, caricature of a man
who never began to know himself.

The power of God is in me.
Listen.

Thousands of Greeks struggled and fought
bravely. Thousands of these thousands died.
For what? Those who died
will never see their children.
No wife came to prepare them
for the grave;
they lie here, all here,
in this foreign, angry earth, this earth that hates
their dead, decaying bones.

At home the same sad story:
women waited, died lonely,
old men longed for sons
who are but poor accursed bones
in nameless, unattended graves,
bad patches of earth
not worthy of a beggar's spit
or the stench of a dead dog in the sun.
These are the things the Greeks have won.
These are the prizes of conquering men.
Men who win wars win nothing.

Listen.

Now, I speak of us.

We are a fighting people
and fighting we died to save our people.
In the mad rage of war
friends bore their dead friends home.
Women's hands washed them,
wrapped them in white shrouds
to lie at peace in their own loved earth.
And while the gentle dead enjoyed
a sweet eternal sleep
their living friends fought on

knowing what they were fighting for
close to their wives and children
in their own land, passionate, at home,
not like the Greeks,
the lost, conquering, joyless Greeks.

And Hector, our dead hero, what is his grief?
Hector is dead, Hector is true and proud
and we all know the great heart he had.
That knowledge is a gift from the Greeks.
Years ago, we hardly knew Hector
or the courage that was in him
but now we know the truth of his blood,
a man loved by his people, loved by his God.

Listen. God is in me. Listen.

People of my heart, do everything you can
to banish war
from the lives of women, men and children.
But if war comes to the land
like a murderous brute into your house
and you find that you must fight
the fight like people who have found
their special light,
there's no evil in that fight.

Therefore, my mother, do not pity the dead
of this great-hearted city.
And do not pity me,
bride of a conquering King.
He'll swell with royal pride to sing
my praises and my charms
locked in his hot, majestic arms.
It is his death
that I will sing.
Love will kill a king, and kill a king, and kill a king.
When he governs me in bed
shall I pray for words to praise him right?
Shall I whisper and sigh and cry in passion?
Or shall I lift the black axe out of the swamp?
Shall I wipe the bloodstains from the blade?
Shall I become the black axe
in my mind, in the bed

159

where Agamemnon rides me in the dark
or in the light?

Randy Agamemnon! Godalmighty fucker Agamemnon!
You are making love to a black axe
covered in bloodstains,
and the black axe feels like the flesh of a woman
chosen to pay homage to your greatness.
Her only problem is to pay that homage right.
Listen, Agamemnon, listen!
Look into my eyes, Agamemnon, look into my eyes:
the war is over, you are the winner, I am your prize.
While you are loving in the dark or in the light
the black axe is singing of your death.
Agamemnon! Listen in the silence of your tired fucker's body
to the song of the black axe.

TALTHYBIUS. (*Breaks the spell she has cast.*)
If I did not know that you are mad,
maddened by the thought
that you must share Agamemnon's bed,
like it or not,
I'd make you swallow your wild words
here and now.

Why in the name of all that's holy,
in the name of hard-won victory,
did Agamemnon choose such a mad creature,
such a perversion of woman's nature?
Yet he has! He has!
My King! My master has chosen
a mad woman before all other women.
Your madness sparks a madness in my King.
Who are you? Where do your words come from?
What do they mean?
Look! I will forget all that you have said!
I will forget every word of praise and blame,
the hate you generate at Agamemnon's name,
I will forget it all.
Come, walk with me. Walk in peace with me,
I'll take you to Agamemnon.
And heaven grant that he may find in you
what he believes he will!
Do the Gods play mocking tricks when Kings pick women?

I'm only a common soldier
a poor man
but I'd never be so daft
so clean out of my head
as to choose a lunatic like this
to share my bed!

(*He pauses, looks at her.*)

Crazy! Crazy! Is Agamemnon crazy too?
Or will he get a special kick
out of fucking a lunatic virgin like you?

(*Goes among women.*)

This creature's mad!
Are you all mad? Are all women mad?
Or are you crafty bitches
waiting to see how the wind blows
and what the sea will bring?

(*Begins to approach various women.*)

You! What's in your head?
You look beaten; but a beaten
woman still plays games.
Even lying in the dirt you
can turn up trumps!

You! What schemes are covered
by your helplessness?
You can't fool me!
You're as moody as the sea,
and as treacherous, if a man's not careful!

And you! And you! And you!
What plans have you?
Are you planning to go mad
so that you can distract a man?
Are you cultivating the lost look,
the hurt look, the beaten look,
the bruised and battered look?

(*He turns to go, then speaks gently to* HECUBA.)

When you are told to do so, go with the men
sent by Odysseus. I have heard

the Queen that you will serve
is a kind, wise woman.
I have heard
that all her thought is sweet and patient
and her ways are gentle.

CASSANDRA.
(*She sees him, the entire scene, for the first time.*)
(*To* TALTHYBIUS.) Slave! You poor, despicable slave
of a go-between!
What would you think
if you had a mind of your own!
What would you do
if you weren't the slave of another man?

(*To* OTHERS.) Slaves! Mother! Voices of death!
The shadow of dead men's agony hovers over all,
the day wears pain like a black jewel
and I can smell the fingers of men
whose hands serve a King of hate.
Your voice is gentle to my mother.
Do you know what you are saying?
My mother must go to Odysseus?
My mother's place is not with Odysseus.
My mother's place is here. Here.

(*To herself.*)
Why do I speak?
Odysseus knows nothing of what waits for him.
His troubles have hardly begun.
A man astray, lost, betrayed,
here and there like a fish in the sea –
the man who plans to bed my mother!
Odysseus is going home.
For ten years he will struggle to go home. Home!
He will taste horror after horror
he will see his own men eaten alive
he will see his own men changed into pigs
he will be battered shipwrecked stupefied
he will see the healing light of the sun
become the voice of his own agony.
He will go to hell, alive to hell,
he will wander the sea
and when he reaches home at last

the door that he has longed to open
will admit him to appalling sorrow.
That is what faces the man
who plans his pleasure with my mother.

And what faces me?
Take me now! Take me to the King,
I shall lie beside the King
…lie beside the King!
King! Lump of dust and blood and muck,
I'll go to your bed.
But there's another bed I see for you –
in a hole somewhere in the ignorant hills
with icy rain forever spitting down.
Dead…outcast…naked as the winter light…
Who is it? – It is I
lying by my King.
All around, I hear them cry,
the wild beasts of the wilderness,
they move in slowly, crying, slowly,
hungry, crying, to where we lie
in bed. The wild beasts watch our bodies
and there from where I lie
beside this thing that calls itself a King
I study the wild beasts. How innocent they are!

(She grips her wreathed head.) Flowers! Flowers!
Flowers of my God breathing his love
into my blood until I feel
the old unkillable joy!
No man can humiliate me forever!

Hell! King of hell!
I'll tear every flower from my head
and pitch it to hell!
O God, these flowers…white, white,
darkness…there was a special light.
If any shred remains, be with me now.
White petal of my heart, be with me now.

(To TALTHYBIUS.*)* Take me to the ships!
I face the sea.
A man's body, important with the power of hell,
walks with me.
A man's body, a winner's body, waits for me.

Mother – Goodbye.
Goodbye, my city.
My sisters and my brother, goodbye,
Goodbye, my father.
No, I am with you all.
Goodbye. I am with you all.
(*To* TALTHYBIUS.) I am ready, slave!

She goes with TALYTHYBIUS *and soldiers.* HECUBA, *motionless a while, falls to the earth.*

WOMAN. Help her!
Help the Queen from the ground!
Raise her up!

Women go to help. She brushes them off, and speaks from the earth.

HECUBA. Here...let me lie here.
Please, please, do not try to help me now.
I know what it means to be nothing,
I have heard voices of nothing call me
to their place of nothingness.
If I call on God for help
all I find is his helplessness.
Yet I must seek and I must cry
for help that seems not to exist.
O let me dream of things long gone
and feel the living presence of the past.
I knew great men, I walked with kings,
now I must lie in a hated bed.
Strong sons I had, the very best
and I was proud to mother them
and I saw them put to death
and I must lie in their killer's bed.

My daughters too! I reared them
for those randy, conquering Greeks.
Not a daughter with me now!
Not a shred of hope is left
that I shall look into their eyes
nor they in mine, ever again.
Women are swept by men who think
that conquest makes them half-divine.
Now I descend into the pit,
a captive slave at my enemies' feet

164

forced to do whatever they wish:
'Open the door! Shut the door!
Grind the wheat! Bake the bread!
Set the table! Sweep the floor!
Lie soft and warm and open your legs!'

A woman must be whatever
a conquering man wishes her to be!

To think that all my life I walked proud and free!

My clothes are torn, my flesh is torn,
humiliation chills my veins, my bones,
and I am sick with shame!

Think of it! Simply that I must lie
in a man's bed, waiting for his pleasure,
my soul repelled, my heart numb with terror,
my mind half-crazy with loathing.
Simply that I must submit
to what freezes my blood with hate,
think what seas have weighed on me,
have poured over me in their ecstacy
and will pour, pour
until I am no more...
And O my dear Cassandra,
daughter I have loved in a way
no music reaches, no word can say,
where have you gone?
What will you become?

And where are you, Polyxena?

And my dear sons, where are you?

How, in so short a time, can this
beautiful world become a world of loss?

And who can help me now,
lying on this ground?
What hope is there?
I am what I am, a slave
who once walked free,
an upright woman in her natural beauty.
But now, I am cast down,
stupid as a stone.

How shall I ever stand again?
I have lost so much
there is nothing left for me to save.
No human can be happy
this side of the grave.

WOMAN. If there's any music left in this world
it is the music of our grief.
Our grief was a huge horse,
his belly packed with death.
It was so beautiful, that horse,
huge and mighty and high,
young women left their homes,
so did all the old men.
Young and old sang and rejoiced in thanksgiving
for the huge beautiful creature
bringing their doom.

Men and women of our city put their eyes upon the horse
and pulled it after them
like a ship they were about to launch
until it stood
on the floor of the stone temple of Pallas Athena.
It stood there on the floor,
the floor that soon would flow with blood.
As the night descended
the people sang and danced
in the shadow of the horse.
Everywhere, torches flared in gratitude.
Even in the darkened houses
the rooms glowed with happiness and joy.
The people's hearts were glad:
had not heaven sent a special gift, a horse,
beautiful and big enough
to bear the weight of all their dreams
and sweep them forward to a future made of hope?
That night, I myself was singing in the choir
before the Temple of the Virgin in the Mountains
when suddenly the city rocked
with cries of havoc and despair
filling the bloody streets of massacre.
Out of the perfect, gigantic horse
Death poured like a black wave over the city,

the symbol of our hope became our doom,
the black wave swallowed everyone in its path,
old men froze in disbelief,
children were struck dumb with terror,
young women in their beds
knew that horror was upon them.
Their warm flesh was ice.
Since that night, the women of this city
have swallowed every horror
the conquering Greeks could dream of.
And believe me, these men dreamed and acted
with an energy so obscene
I ask myself, what is a woman?
How much abuse can a woman take,
how much horror can a woman endure
before she ceases to be a woman,
before she ceases to be human?
Will the day come when she won't be human?

WOMAN. No woman is anything now.
    Women are dead. We are all dead
    and being dead we may become
    the grass that grows between stones.
    Or we may become the tears
    that you have cried in the past
    for some inexplicable sense of waste,
    some insult you suffered or threw
    at some man in a public place
    because he stared into your face
    as if he'd know you in a way
    you could never know yourself.

    All women are dead of shame tonight
    and being dead we may cry
    for the suffering of our city,
    for the hungry in our midst,
    the lonely in our rooms,
    the sprawled outcasts in our streets
    the lost in doors and laneways,
    the dumb in the pity of shadows,
    the mad in the isolation of themselves.

    Women, we are become this city,
    we are become its untold loss,

its forgotten truths, commemorated lies,
its unspoken and unwritten history,
its guilty silences and echoing scandals,
its tiny gestures forgotten soon as made
its winters learning how to smile
its summers renewing the old chill
its mornings laughing
like girls thrilling to their first love.

What can our city ever be
but we
in this poverty
worse than death?

But they will bring us back from death –
our conquerors!

And we must go and lie with them –
our conquerors!
And we must be
the mothers of the children of our enemies.

Our children – the children of our enemies!

Who knows anything of love or hate
or joy or grief or callousness or pity?

All we know is that
we are our city.

Our broken, fallen, ridiculed city.

Enter ANDROMACHE, *with her son.*

WOMAN. Andromache!
Where are you going?

ANDROMACHE. To a Greek's bed.

HECUBA. One more hell
And one more woman in it!

ANDROMACHE. Your word describes my heart.

HECUBA. Hell is the air we breathe.

ANDROMACHE. You have yours.

HECUBA. Yes.

ANDROMACHE. You are lost – alone.

HECUBA. Yes. And my city is lost – alone.
    And plundered.

ANDROMACHE. Most savagely raped.

HECUBA. Dead children.

ANDROMACHE. Shattered streets of sorrow.

HECUBA. These streets are me.

ANDROMACHE. I want my lover.
    Give me my lover.

HECUBA. Your lover's dead.
    His flesh is black earth,
    not for your flesh now or ever.

ANDROMACHE. Protect me. Where is my love?

HECUBA. Where is my love? O my love
    let me be with you, where are you,
    O my love?

ANDROMACHE. I could lift my heart out of my breast,
    search every corner of it
    for one small sign
    of love that lived there,
    like my children in my house
    so happy
    I tremble to remember.

HECUBA. Do not remember. Do not remember.

ANDROMACHE. If I banish children from my head
    A burning city flames instead.

HECUBA. I am criss-cross streets of fire.

ANDROMACHE. Dead men lie naked,
    vultures croak for joy
    because the criss-cross fiery streets
    are the death of Troy.
    Love staggers here and there,
    raggedy flesh, mad eyes,
    starved hands flailing the air
    packed with cries.

169

HECUBA. Home! My home!
  The end is come.

FIRST WOMAN. Can Hecuba cry?
  Is she frozen within?

ANDROMACHE. What do you see?

HECUBA. I see God's hand
  killing my land.

ANDROMACHE. Hooves of maddened cattle
  are pounding my head.

HECUBA. We're helpless.
  They've taken Cassandra.

ANDROMACHE. There's worse to come.

HECUBA. Is it possible?

ANDROMACHE. Polyxena is dead, her body
  thrown on Achilles' grave.

HECUBA. That's what Talthybius said,
  I didn't understand.

ANDROMACHE. I touched her body where it lay,
  I wept for her.

HECUBA. *(To herself.)* Beyond imagining!
  Beyond enduring!
  Who can imagine such evil?
  My daughter's body thrown on a Greek's grave
  like a flower in the gutter.

ANDROMACHE. Polyxena is dead, free
  of the misery where we are trapped.

HECUBA. Death is not life.
  Death is nothing, less than nothing.
  Life laughs at death.

ANDROMACHE. Better to be dead
  than living horribly.
  To be dead is to be
  beyond the reach of pain
  and consciousness of wrong.
  But a living woman

bullied from joy to sorrow,
pity her, for she is lost
to her old self: and every moment of her life
is raw with knowledge of her loss.
Her life is like a wound that cannot heal.
Your dead daughter is like an unborn child.
Polyxena is dead, knowing nothing
of the man who killed her
or of his lust for her.

It is well for any woman
to consider the nature of a man's lust.
I did.

I noted and considered why men praise women.
Aware of the reasons for their praise
I did everything to please my man,
Hector. I realised that always,
whatever a woman's motives may be,
straight or twisted, dark or in the light,
innocent or guilty, wrong or right,
to try her hand with another man
puts her immediately in a dubious light.
So I stayed at home and walked in my own garden.
I did not allow into my home
the kind of woman
who delights in giving another woman
a bad name.
The glinting knives of gossiping tongues
never even scratched me.
I thought my own thoughts
and found they were enough.
When Hector came to me
he found me bright and peaceful.
I gave him what his heart desired,
hearing, always what he had to say.
I became a gifted listener, patient, sympathetic.
In my husband's presence,
I had a quiet tongue and a pleasant face.
I understood him, I understood myself,
and so I created a fair, effective way of living;
I knew when to insist
and when to obey.

I never resorted to any evil guile,
I created a life
with my own, deliberate style.
I created the space in which his vanity might move
like a beautiful, confident cat.

I created peace.
And then this peace became my enemy.
The Greek, Achilles' son, hearing of my peace,
chose me.
Now I must serve the killer of my husband.
I must lie in the bed of my husband's murderer.
But how shall I serve such a man?
Shall I forget
my Hector's handsome face
and open up my heart
to this new master?

Shall I betray the dead
whom I was glad to serve?
And how shall I feel
when I am fucked by his murderer
in that murderer's bed?
And if in bed I shrink
from the embrace of this fresh lover
will he beat me, cripple me,
or strike me dead in rage?

After all, I'm only a slave.
If I'm a slave, shall I think like a slave?
And what does that mean – thinking like a slave?

Men who have studied their own lust
will tell you
that a single night in a man's arms
will tame the wildest woman.
Shame! My thoughts begin to shame me.
Can a woman's lips so soon forget
her dead
and quickly love the lust in a stranger's bed?
Who can blame the woman that –
her husband in his grave –
explores the unknown possibilities of love?
Will not a lively mare run on, run on

to another stallion, when her mate is gone?
O my dead Hector, most loved of men
who, all alive, was mine and only mine,
my love, my prince, my man, my perfect majesty,
no man had ever touched me
when you strode masterfully into my life
and masterfully took me for your wife.
And you are dead, Hector, dead
as yesterday's love;
and I must be
a slave and take my chances on the sea
and be the kind of woman
that a man will say I have to be.
And yet I clearly see
that if my body is a slave
an untouched portion of my mind is free.
To be a slave and free at once – how can this be?
I am a woman; men will put me on the sea.
And yet, no matter where I am, I still must think of me.

What does dead Polyxena
for whom you weep
know of the twists and turns of her own mind? Nothing!
What does she know of mad frantic inexplicable dreams
that leave her mind and body
exhausted in the light of dawn?
Nothing! Nor does she need to know.
My mind is crookeder and wilder
than any dream I've ever had.
I have no hope; I know I have no hope.
Nor will I lie to myself in my private hell
pretending that my plight is well,
or fairly well.
And yet, I dream. Some dreams are sweet,
even a slave will dream. Somewhere, a special light
burns for me, for you, for all lost women…
A good dream to a slave
is a crust of bread to a starving beggar.
Better a good dream than a futile pain in the heart.

FIRST WOMAN. You have already gone where I must go.
You know completely what I must try to know.

HECUBA. Look at the ships.
I have heard that when a storm comes
each man does his best to face it
and if the sea wins
the men surrender
to the conquering storm.
I surrender to my own grief,
I don't struggle, I don't curse the sea
or strive to make things be
other than the way they have to be.
Over me they pour, the waves, great waves of misery.

God's overwhelming waves are drowning me!
My child, let Hector sleep.
You may weep
till the eyes melt from your head.
Your weeping will not bring him from the dead.
Keep the unstained beauty of your eyes
for the man you'll sleep with soon.
Be gentle, modest, dutiful and wise
and win this man. Be a winner, Andromache.
Go eagerly to bed with this new man
and let your body teach
you how to win.
When you let him lose himself in you,
there's nothing that you cannot gain.
He thinks you're his slave;
you know he's yours.
Now, you have your master in your power,
help those who love you and whom you love.
Your conqueror is conquered by your guile,
he cannot distinguish his own fulfilment from your style.
The poor, blind winner!
Rear this child among your enemies,
Hector's child, that he may grow
among his enemies in mastery
and hope and strength. One day,
he'll help again, when stone on stone is laid,
to build a city that will restore our pride
and our own loved ways of living.
O how my mind is leaping, leaping,
thought chasing thought like athletes running
before the cheering people on a summer's evening.

174

My thoughts are swifter now
than any sword flashing in a man's hand!
But who is this?
Talthybius! Again, Talthybius!

Enter TALTHYBIUS *with soldiers. He's upset.*

TALTHYBIUS. Andromache! Hector's wife!
Brave wife of the bravest man in Troy,
I have no joy in telling you this.
The people and the Kings have all agreed to...

ANDROMACHE. There's evil on your lips.
Speak it.

TALTHYBIUS. Your child –

ANDROMACHE. Yes?

TALTHYBIUS. Your son will never see you
serve another man;
your son's voice will never speak
in obedience to a Greek.

ANDROMACHE. Good!
Will they leave him here
to re-build this old city
of his father, mother, sisters, brothers,
ancestors?

TALTHYBIUS. The people...the Kings...

ANDROMACHE. If you have bad news to tell,
tell it now. Why can't you speak? Why? Speak!

TALTHYBIUS. Your son must die.

ANDROMACHE. I can sleep in my enemy's bed.
But my son – dead!
My son – murdered by the Greeks.
Dead!

TALTHYBIUS. Odysseus, speaking before everyone,
argued eloquently that –

ANDROMACHE. Lost! My son! My city! Lost!

TALTHYBIUS. Odysseus argued and Odysseus won.
He said that the son of Hector,

the son of one so brave and threatening
should not be allowed to grow to manhood –

ANDROMACHE. May his own words
    curse the lives of his own sons.
    May they never grow to men
    but be forever
    dead, forgotten boys.
    May Odysseus be cursed forever.

TALTHYBIUS. Odysseus argued and Odysseus won.
    He said your boy must be flung
    from the topmost heights
    of the walls of Troy.
    Let it be done – now.
    No waiting! No thinking!
    You are a brave woman in great pain,
    do not look for strength no man or God
    can give you.
    Look around you here.
    Is there hope or help or refuge anywhere?
    Your city is taken
    your man is dead
    you are alone and weak, a woman alone,
    a prisoner alone, one woman, a slave.
    How can you resist or fight
    or struggle for even a moment?
    I beg you, Andromache, do not struggle,
    I do not want to see you hurt
    Or wounded, your blood among the stones…

    Why are your lips
    moving in silence? Are you cursing the ships
    and every Greek they bear?
    If I hear one evil word from you
    your son will get no burial
    but be flung broken and naked –
    O my God! Peace!
    Andromache! Peace!
    Bear this misfortune as you have borne
    all your troubles.
    This is war, woman. You must live with war
    and the terrible consequences of war,
    live with war, bear it and bury your child.

If you learn to live with this
no Greek will deepen your loss.
They will recognise your courage.
Andromache, this boy must be flung from the battlements.

ANDROMACHE. You must die, my child,
you must die at the hands of pitiless men,
leaving me alone.
Your father was too brave:
that's why the Greeks are killing you.
His bravery was such
the Greeks fear it in you. They know
that while you live your father is not dead.
Your father's bravery saved the lives of others.
Now, it is the cause of your death.
If you live...you are your father.
O my son, my son!
Kiss me, my son!

The sea...the city in my head.
O God! When I went to Hector's bed
I was a girl in love with a brave man,
brave enough to challenge the world
and the bravest in it. I have no art,
no language to speak of your dead father's
bravery of heart.
There was no end to his daring...
My son, why are you crying?
Why? Why? You cannot know your father.
Your father will not come
your father will not come
not once, not even once,
his sword splitting the grave itself
to set you free.
No, my son, your father will not come.

Your death? How will it happen?
The Greeks will throw you from the city walls.
Down, down through the air
that brought sweet life to our city and its people,
down through the air you'll plunge –
my God, your body, my son's body,
your back, your head, your neck,
your neck that I have kissed

and kissed and touched and lingered over –
and there's no pity!
And is it for nothing, nothing at all
that I have reared you?
Is it to see your body
pitched from a great height
to break on the earth
that I nursed you through long sickness,
watching over you till I felt
old and withered with watching,
my head falling in unwilling sleep,
forcing myself awake
that I might not miss one moment watching you.
Kiss me, my son
kiss me once
and never again.
Put your arms about my neck,
my son, my brave Hector's son,
your arms about my neck
and kiss me, kiss me, your lips
into my lips –
You Greeks,
you are torturing me
as no woman has ever been tortured.
A child, why murder a child,
an innocent child? And will I witness it?

At the back of all this – a woman.
Helen, may every curse
that ever issued
from the mind of God and man
blast and savage your heart
and every part of your body
until the rats and vampires of the world
fear to come near you.
May sickness and disease
scar and madden your beautiful eyes
and may your name be hated by children
until the world howls
to its miserable end.
Helen, you are not human.
You are the daughter of many fathers,
evil, hate, murder, death,

every monster prowling the earth.
Helen, you are killing my son.
in your lovely eyes
I see my son falling to his death.

(She gives her son to TALTHYBIUS.*)*

Quick! Take him! Drag him to the wall!
Throw him from the highest point!
Smash him in such pieces
I cannot recognise him.
Men, beasts, take him, break him,
be quick, this is war, be quick,
live with war, be quick, see, I do not resist,
I am more impotent than any old man,
I am a helpless woman, woman alone, alone.
Throw him, crack flesh, break bone,
I cannot lift a hand to help the boy,
throw me from the highest wall,
scatter me under the ships,
my coward's body will disgust the sea.

(She faints, half-rises, then −)

Quick! I must go to a Greek's bed!
My son is dead, this is war,
there must be love somewhere. Dead.

The soldiers close around her.

FIRST WOMAN. For Helen's kiss,
for one vile woman's kiss
we have come to this!
Thousands of young men are dead
because of one woman's hateful bed.
Helen! Is Helen human?

TALTHYBIUS *bends over her and takes the child from her.*

TALTHYBIUS. Child, let your mother go.
Come with me
to the towering walls above
your father's city.

There you will meet your death
− Hold! Hold him! Hold him tight! −

179

Why must I, who love child-brightness,
quench this light?

Why must I end a life
that has hardly begun?
Why must I kill an innocent
when the war is won?

Would to heaven some other man
did what I must do.
To kill a child! Is this my glory?
No more! Do it! Now!

HECUBA. Child, you are my son's son
and these Greeks are killing you.
They have stripped me of everything.
What can I offer you?

Take my battered heart,
take my beaten head,
these are the gifts I offer you
on your way to the dead,

the last gifts in my power to give.
Nothing lives but pain.
As long as I breathe I will say this
again and again –

Our city is a city of pain
our days are days of pain
Is there any end to human pain?
Are there any words for the final pain?
(She breaks down.)

The child breaks free from TALTHYBIUS, *starts back to his mother, is
grabbed by a soldier.* ANDROMACHE *is dragged off to the ships – cries
of 'To the ships! To the ships! – and* TALTHYBIUS *takes the child.*

WOMAN. A child is taken to his death,
a woman dragged to shame.
That's how a city dies.

Silent houses break up inside.
Ships' bellies are crammed with women.
That's how a city dies.

Who has time for broken things?

180

Or ghosts? Or stories of things done and said
by men and women long with the dead?
That's how a city dies.

Women stolen away by sea
are prizes, prizes –
something no fighting man denies.

And what is love? And where is love?
We have grown so used to murder
we no longer hear the cries.
Love is murdered here today.
That's how a city dies.

King MENELAUS *enters, with soldiers.*

MENELAUS. I cannot imagine a more perfect day!
I am about to see the woman that I –
No, I haven't come here for her.
I came for the man
who ate and drank with me
and stole my woman.
But Paris is long dead
battered to pieces by the hooves
of good Greek horses.
Today I want to see –
Curse the bitch! She was my wife
and I can hardly bring myself
to say her name.
She's with the prisoners here
in one of these huts,
here, among the women-slaves.
The men who fought to win her
have given her to me
to do with as I will. Imagine! As I will!
Shall I take her for pleasure
here, now, right here, even now?
Or pretend to kill her?
And get a little pleasure from her fear?
Or shall I take her home?
Shall I take Helen home?
Home! No, I'll not kill Helen here.
I'll take her home across the sea
and there hand her over to these families

who've lost their young men fighting for her.
They'll think of ways to deal with her.
Soldiers! Go into these huts,
drag out that bitch from where she's crouching
in some stinking corner.
Find her, drag her out here,
pull her by that famous blood-drenched hair
thousands of young Greeks have died for,
and drag her here before me, here,
before my very eyes –

(He controls himself.)

And when a favourable wind will come
my ships will take her home.

The soldiers approach a hut to force the door, second hut on the left.

HECUBA. Whoever you are,
    ruler of every star and every river
    beat of every creature's heart
    maker and sustainer of all living things
    the blood that courses and the voice that sings
    of dreams born in solitude,
    God,
    I praise you now with all my being,
    seeing
    that justice strides into our midst
    when all seemed lost.

MENELAUS. That is a strange prayer.
    (Turning.) Who spoke these words to heaven?

HECUBA. Do not look long in Helen's eyes.
    If you look into her eyes
    you will drown
    as surely as a drunken man
    staggering alone at night
    through a treacherous swamp will drown
    in the sneering light of the moon.
    If you look into her eyes
    and surrender to what you see
    or think you see
    you will forget who you are
    and the purpose of your coming here.

Your anger will seem strange to you.
You will no longer feel the need for vengeance.
You will not be then
the man you are now.
If you look deep in Helen's eyes
your sense of yourself
will melt like a candle
in the depth of night.
And what use is a melted self,
a helpless lump of wax that Helen
using her old magical skill
will shape, manipulate according to her will?
She traps strong men
she poisons homes
she steals men's hearts
she snares great cities
she is a cup of magic;
drink it
you will drown in her,
you are hers forever,
lost to yourself
trapped in adoration of her eyes,
her lips, her face, her hair,
yes, you will find Helen here.
Do I not know her?
Do you not know her?
All these, do they not know her
the eloquent, evil, beautiful Queen
of all that women know to be obscene
and men cannot, will not, or refuse to recognise?

The soldiers return with HELEN, *gentle, composed, unafraid.*

HECUBA. Menelaus, when you look in Helen's eyes,
Think of her victims!

MENELAUS. You are my prize.

HECUBA. Listen to her, Menelaus. Hear her out
and when she has spoken
let me answer.
You know nothing of the wrongs and horrors
she unleashed in this city.
Hear her story and you'll know why

this cool, manipulating bitch must die.
But as you listen to her story, beware of her tongue.

MENELAUS. Helen's story! A waste of breath and time
and yet for your sake, Hecuba, I'll hear her out.
I have no mercy for her, but let her speak!

HELEN. (*Points to* HECUBA.) Blame this woman!
This woman started it all!
She gave birth to Paris,
the man who stole me from you.
Out of her womb sneaked the thief
of your happiness.
Before the birth, Hecuba dreamed
she had a firebrand in her womb.
She knew she was the mother of destruction.

Look at her now!
Shall we call her a woman?
Or a tyrant judge, rigid with accusation,
lusting for my blood?
Or a twisted bitter jealous thing
poisoned by memory?
Or a bad lump of envy
raging for lost beauty?
Who is this woman
who cannot wait to scream for my death?

Why did I leave you, Menelaus?
I was stolen by Paris, the firebrand in her womb.
Paris saw me, loved me, stole me away.
For my beauty I was captured
and brought across the sea.
Do not blame me for my beauty.
My beauty should have been the reason
why my people love me
as I loved you, a reasonable man.

But why did I leave you, Menelaus?
Why did I run away with another man?
Paris came, Paris the firebrand came,
a goddess came with him, with Paris
whom you welcomed to your house
and left alone with me.
You left me alone with a firebrand!

Remember that
when it comes to handing out the blame.
Blame! Hecuba blames me
for the evil she launched on the world,
she blames me for her misery.

These other women blame me for theirs.
Yet Hecuba and all these women
encouraged their men to fight
and when they lost
they pitched their blame on me.

There must always be someone to blame, Menelaus.
At home, men and women blame me for their dead,
for all the young men lost in this long war.
Why do they go to war?
They go to war to fuck each other to death
and then the daisies sprout laughing from their corpses.
The mad absurdity of it all!
Tens of thousands play war's murderous game
and when the game is over
and the dead must be buried,
the maimed and crippled comforted,
the women chosen for the winners' beds,
someone must be blamed
for what had to happen
because men must sink their swords
in the backs and bellies of other men.
Think, Menelaus, think!
Your knife is deep in the flesh of another man,
he's screaming, screaming,
your knife goes deeper,
deeper than you've ever been in any woman,
deeper than you've ever been in me.
Listen! His screams are changing,
becoming whispers,
your knife is cutting the throats of fear and shame.
No, Menelaus, no! I am not to blame!

You left Paris alone with me
and took to the open sea,
away from me, away, away from me,
leaving Paris alone with me.

Do you know what it means to be alone?
Alone as a mad woman
who in her madness
has moments when she knows she is not mad?
Alone as a cry for help too obvious to be heard?
Alone as a whisper in a sick room?
Would you rather go to war
than be alone?
Would you rather sink your sword
in the back or belly of another man?
Menelaus, are you grateful to your God
for the mad spilling of young men's blood?
Blood, Menelaus, blood and the screams of the dying
are preferable to the silent screams of being alone.

You are far away from me now,
lost at the other side of the sea.
Have you ever looked at me,
praised me,
touched me?
I am here, I think my own strange thoughts,
stranger than the screams of the dying
or the murderous lust of the living,
the obscene obviousness of war?
Would you like to look into my mind
and surprise yourself with what you find?
You know my body, Menelaus; now I offer you my mind
where I find this question: why did I forget
my love, my land, my family and friends
to sail the sea with a strange man?

Surely it was not I,
not I alone (how should I ever dare?)
but the goddess standing at Paris's side
that prompted me to go!

Surely it was not I, but she.
If you must punish anyone
for the fact that I am here
and not at home with you, my Lord,
then punish her who prompted him
who prompted me to run away
from all that I held dear.

Yes, I did wrong
but I did wrong because of her.

I am not to blame.

You know my body, Menelaus.
Here is my mind again.
This is your question: why,
when Paris at last was dead and buried,
and I was freed from the spell
cast by the goddess,
why did I still stay in his house?
Why did I not escape to the Greek ships
and be safe among my own people,
be with you, dear Menelaus? Alone with you?

I tried, I tried,
so many times I tried, but all in vain!
That old gate-guardian was the man
who thwarted every attempt I made
to reach the ships. I was watched,
Menelaus, watched night and day.
Day and night I plotted my escape,
waiting always for the golden moment.
It never came. The guards and sentinels
knew of my intention to escape
and more than once they tied me to a rope
and dangled me from the battlements.
But still I kept my hope
that one day I'd escape
and go where I belonged:
in your house, Menelaus, in your gracious house.
Alone with you, Menelaus.

My husband, you have heard my story.
How can you kill me
who never meant you a moment's harm?
Calm the storm in your mind.
Think quietly. Listen!
I was stolen from you.
I did not leave you.
I suffered misery and pain
at the hands of a strange man.

I use my own words
to speak my own truth.

If you choose to kill me for my truth
then kill me: but know
it is Helen's truth you kill
to your eternal shame.
Truth-killer Menelaus – may that never be your name.
Your name is sweeter far than that,
Menelaus, reasonable man, lover of justice,
patient listener to a pleading voice,
Helen's voice,
Helen who loved you truly
in your own house.

MENELAUS. Thousands of young men are dead –
and you are not to blame?

HELEN. No! I am not to blame!
As Helen is my name
I swear to heaven I am not to blame!
What did any single one
of all these thousands of young men who died
know of *me*?
That war was fought
in furious ignorance by ignorant men!
Not one, not one who died, knew *me*!

They knew as much of me
as they did of whatever lives or dies
at the bottom of the sea!
And why must you blame me, my beauty,
my leaving your bed for another man?
Why blame me
for your own pride, your own bafflement,
your need to own me?
Nobody owns me.
Do not blame me, Menelaus,
love me for my truth.
Look into my eyes,
listen to my voice,
we are together again, we are living
together in the warm house of our love.
Look into my eyes

listen to my voice
this is my skin, my flesh, my face, my hair.
These are my hands, reaching out to you forever.
Touch me, touch me, there, there...
Touch me, you will recover everything you've lost.
Touch me, you will know again the man you really are.
When you touch me, you are following your true star.

WOMAN. Break her spell, Hecuba, break her spell!
Her voice is heaven but her heart is hell.
She is eloquent, evil, beautiful, vile!
She makes me so afraid! Break her spell!

HECUBA. Helen is a liar! She lives to lie!
Lies spring more quickly from her lips
than evil glances from a demon's eye.
Helen has lied her way through life
and cannot cease to lie until she dies.
Everything within her and about her
is a lie. The greatest lie of all
is her beauty. She uses it to get her way.
That is Helen's truth – getting her way!
That's why she blames a goddess
for her own icy lust
as men blame God
for their own pathetic failures.
Outrageous, smiling, lying bitch!
Getting your way through lies!
Do you think you have the power
to deceive not only Menelaus,
not only me, Hecuba,
but all of us women
who have seen you fawning for years,
smiling, cheating, lying, deceiving for years,
getting your way
with beauty and with style.

My God! The hideous simplicity
of complex women!

My son was beautiful.
Paris was a handsome prince of a man.
You didn't have to look at him twice,
Helen, to know that.

Beauty has an eye for beauty.
Your beauty hides the mind
of a manipulating bitch, the kind of bitch
men trample on each other to get near,
the kind of low bitch
who must be always at the top.
In you, Helen, the stink of evil
is a personal perfume.
When you saw Paris
your lying heart began its charming war.
First, you charmed yourself
and then him.

When you saw his youth and beauty,
his vigorous, magnetic fire,
you wanted him to add to you,
to increase your beauty, deepen your desire,
fire the passion that was dying
in the comfortable house of Menelaus.
You were growing listless, Helen, bored and listless
because you'd got your way with Menelaus.
A bored, beautiful woman is a monster.
You are the most beautiful monster
the world has known.

So Paris took you – by force, of course!
And you were brave, resisting to the end!
Yet no one heard your cries for help!
It was night, I know, and people slept
while you, poor captive, whimpered and wept
for your lost darling Menelaus!

Then when you came to Troy,
and quietly sat among your lovely lies
and men died everywhere for you,
you played it both ways.

One day it was 'Paris, O my love,
O my dear, unequalled man,
no woman dares to love you as I can.'
And the next moment –
'Where is Menelaus?
Where is my loving lord
who understood my every little word?'

How you suffered, Helen!
How your heart split in two
while young men in their thousands
died for you!
But you know that's what men are for:
they fight and work and laugh and sometimes cry.
Pick one, Helen. Pick a man. Fuck him. Let him die.
Stick him in a grave, cold, deep, far from the sun.
And remember always – take care of number one.
Remember when I tried to help you escape?
I said, 'I will get you back to your own people
and my people will have peace at last,'
and you replied that I was talking like a traitor,
like an enemy of my own people.

And you were concerned for my people!
Why not?
Servants tended you, bowed to you,
your every whim was satisfied,
every wish granted,
every lie swallowed as a child
will swallow promises.

And now, you come out here,
brazen-beautiful as ever,
you dare to stand there
in my presence, before my eyes
and – I can't believe it! – spin your lies
to get your way.
How can such evil
have such a perfect style?

You should have crawled out here
like the beast you are
dressed in the stinking rags and tatters
that show your heart.
You should be trembling here,
your head should be cropped of that hair,
you should know yourself for the guilty thing you are.
But no, you are Helen still, and therefore
a liar to the end!
Helen, you are whatever
turns a man into a murderer,
you created the thought of rape,

you are the cause of all our torture
and you will not escape!

King Menelaus, it's time for justice.
Kill her!
Kill her and let others live.
Think of what she said, of what I've said.
Now is the time for justice
for the woman who betrayed your bed.
Kill her, now! Now!
Be urgent as you are wise.
Kill her! Then make a law for women everywhere:
Whatever woman betrays her husband, dies!

HELEN. (*To* HECUBA.) You look at me as if you'd never seen
a woman in your life.

HECUBA. Yes. A woman. But what do I see in you?

HELEN. What do you see?

HECUBA. I see a cunt. I see an evil cunt.
It's all you are. Your answer to everything.
The only thing you have to offer to the world.
You use what you are to be more than you are.
Men exist to help you do that.

HELEN. What else do you see?

HECUBA. I see a greedy, scheming bitch
who wants to take, take, take
till she's grabbed everything and everybody
for herself.

HELEN. What else do you see?

HECUBA. I see a traitor, not only of men
but of women.
Treachery is written on your skin.

HELEN. What else do you see?

HECUBA. I see an animal that knows when to strike and kill,
that knows also when to be passive
and slink away into the silence of herself.

HELEN. What else do you see?

HECUBA. I see a woman who can act
     whatever part she chooses.
     We women play one part, one part alone.
The circling women become more and more enraged. They throw insults
like stones at HELEN.

WOMEN *circling, shout and scream the following:*

     Thousands of young men dead!
     Homes destroyed!
     Families broken!
     Blood spilled!
     Broken bodies!
     Broken minds!
     Broken hearts.
     You broke them!
     You broke the homes!
     You killed the young men!
     You gave your body to get your way!
     You cheated!
     Lied!
     Stole!
     Left one man for another!
     You wanted everything!
     Everything! For yourself!
     You're an insult to women!
     You mock what we are!
     You're a disgrace!
     A shame!
     Traitor!
     Double-dealer!
     Schemer!
     Nothing matters to you!
     Except what pleases you!
     Scum!
     Trash!
     Swamp!
     Shit!
     Muck!
     Pricktease!
     Wagon!
     Cocksucker!
     Cow!

Sow!
Vixen!
Hustler!
Tart!
Trollop!
Hussy!
Doxy!
Minx!
Rotten fish!
Bag o' crap!
Witch!
Bitch!
Whore!
Slave!

HECUBA. Cunt!

WOMAN. Death to Helen!
Death to the traitor!
King Menelaus, let your judgement
be fair and strong.
It's clear to all the world
Helen has done a dreadful wrong
but it would be a far more dreadful wrong
to let her live!
Kill her! Kill her!

The other women continue to circle HELEN, *hissing-chanting 'Kill her!*
Kill her!' During all this, HELEN *remains calm.*

MENELAUS. (*Turns furiously on* HELEN.)
Get out of here! Men and women
are waiting for you with stones.
You made corpses of their sons,
you filled their hearts with skeletons.
These men and women,
face their hate and rage on every road,
at every window, every door;
and when your body's broken by the stones of hate
you will dishonour me no more.
Get out! You fooled me for too long.
You cannot reach me with your lying tongue.

HELEN. (*Kneels before him, embraces him.*)
I wrap my arms about your knees

194

as I was happy to embrace your body
and will be happy, if you wish, again.
Judge me for who I am.
Helen, your Helen, Helen is who I am, nobody but Helen,
remember that. How can you kill me?

HECUBA. Remember the young men she murdered,
young men who fought at your side,
deception is the blood in her body.
Remember that body in another's bed.
If you don't kill her now
and put that body beyond the bodies of men
you'll be her victim once again.
As long as Helen breathes,
Helen will deceive.

MENELAUS. Peace, Hecuba, peace!
If I do not kill her now
it's not for her sake.
Helen is nothing to me,
nothing…almost nothing.

(*To the soldiers.*) Take her to the shore.
Prepare a ship for her.
She's ready for the sea.

HECUBA. Don't go in the same ship with her.

MENELAUS. Why?

HECUBA. No man who has ever loved Helen
can be sure he will not do so again.
Her evil magic never fails with men.

MENELAUS. Let some other ship take her then.
When we reach home
she will be welcomed by her doom,
black doom, black as her heart.
When women see what Helen must endure
they will be faithful for evermore.
This will not be easy
but the sight of Helen in her blood,
her body bruised and broken
in shreds of meat a man might throw to dogs
will freeze the wandering dreams of women
and keep them in the beds where they belong.

Helen's body, gashed and hacked by stones,
will chill the marrow of the wildest women's bones.
The sight of Helen's blood will do some good,
the body of this vile whore will please the eyes of God.

Exit MENELAUS, *after* HELEN, *escorted by soldiers.*

HECUBA. Will she live or die?
Will she sink in shame and pain
or will the old magic work again?
What does she *do* to men?
What demon helps her to get her way
and yet make men believe her only wish
is to do as they say?
Her style, the gift of hell,
twists men to her design
and yet persuades them all is well,
as if she really is what she but seems.
She makes men feel she is their slave
but she remains the queen of all their dreams.

WOMAN. Laughter is dead as our nights of joy,
the passion of every blessing and every prayer,
the towers and houses, the bread of Troy
the moons of love and hope in the air.
My heart cries, God of the tolerant sky
what did we ever mean in your mind?
Our fabulous city, about to die.
Our people, all, dead leaves in the wind.

HECUBA. Give the dead a chance.

WOMAN. My man is dead.
I go to the long ships,
a stranger's bed
a stranger's lips.

HECUBA. These lips will bring you hope
if you listen to everything they say.
Listen! Listen! And you'll find a way.
Learn from your oppressor!

WOMAN. My children cry for me,
but I must go from them forever.
Where? Where beyond the sea?
What city? Village? Town?

196

Who will sleep with me?
What sort of man
waits for me out there?
Is his heart cruel or kind?
Will he set my mind at ease?
Will he drive me out of my mind?
Will I wander here and there
calling my children's names aloud?
How long will they remember me?
Or will the morning dawn at last
when they won't give a thought to me?
I cannot forget my past.
I'll take it with me on the sea!

HECUBA. The past is richness and waste.

WOMAN. Far out in the waste of the sea
where as a slave I go
I ask one favour of you,
God whom I do not know –
Strike me dead on that sea
where my master's arrogant breath
offends me and strengthens my prayer
for the gift of death.

WOMAN. I have failed! I have failed!

HECUBA. You have not failed!
There is no such thing as failure!
There's only something that you haven't learned,
something that you cannot see.

WOMAN. May I see Helen there,
the blight of all our lives,
may vermin infest her hair,
may the curses of daughters and wives
wither her hands and face.
May poison shrivel her guts
may she never know one hour's peace
from the busy teeth of rats.
May the cold of death assail her
and every pain known to man,
may her womb blacken with cancer
and cancer eat her brain
till she staggers, a reeling idiot

197

from bed to rutting bed
with lovers whose touch is leprosy
whose flesh is both lusty and dead.

Enter TALTHYBIUS, *one or two soldiers,* TALTHYBIUS *carrying the dead child,* ASTYNAX.

WOMAN. A dead boy.
Is there no end to the misery of Troy?

TALTHYBIUS. Andromache is gone, her master's prize:
Andromache who brought tears to my eyes
with her words about her country,
her city and her man, Hector.
She asked me that her son be buried
with proper rites.
Here is Hector's shield.
Andromache requested
that this shield cover her son's body.
She asked me to place the boy
in your hands, Hecuba.
Let him be dressed in whatever clothes
are left to you.
She cannot do these things herself.
Her master won't allow it.
From now on,
she has no choices of her own.
As soon as the boy's body is dressed
we will bury him in the earth
and then set sail.
Do this quickly,
let there be no delay,
quickly, as you've been told.
One thing you need not do, however.
Some distance back I passed a river,
I washed the body in the water,
I cleaned his wounds...
a boy's body...

I will go out now and dig his grave.
Go, do your work, dress the body
and return immediately.
Then, at last, I will be free
to make my way to the waiting sea.
Go.

He goes out with soldiers, leaving the boy's body in HECUBA*'s arms.*

HECUBA. Put Hector's great shield here,
    near me, on the ground.
    Look at it. The Greeks knew fear
    whenever they saw that shield,
    wielded by the bravest man of all.
    Did Hector ever murder a child?
    It takes a Greek to do that.
    Even for Greeks, this was a strange murder.
    Why were they so afraid
    that one day this boy might restore
    his country's pride?
    We are beaten, lashed, smashed into the ground,
    our men are dead, our women slaves,
    our city burnt, our fields destroyed,
    our hearts broken, our bodies weary –
    and the Greeks murder a boy!

    Is innocence to be more feared
    than strength?
    What a death they gave you, boy!
    If you had grown
    and fought and fallen like a man
    then we could have spoken of you
    as we do of the blessèd dead.
    Your eyes saw the world
    you breathed the good air
    you did not get the chance to live
    the full, rich life that was your due.

    Thrown from the walls of your own city!

    Broken! All broken!

    Your head, your hands, shoulders, neck:
    broken.
    So this is it, the end of all:
    a child's crushed skull!
    Death grins out of your face!

    I watched over you in sleep.
    I played with you,
    the daft and giddy games you loved.
    I fell asleep with you,

I woke and looked at you.
We played again.

Grown men feared you!
Ah! The stupid, murderous fear of grown men!

Child, there's nothing left in Hector's house,
nothing left but Hector's shield.
It will cover your body.
Your father's hand gripped that shield
and he was feared.
Now it will cover you
with all we know of love.

(*To the women.*) Go, bring whatever clothes remain.
I am sorry I have so little to give you
and yet I give you all I can.
How vain, how vain are men
who rob and plunder
and think they'll always be
rulers of the land and of the sea.
Vain men! Vain men!
O my broken child of Troy!

Women approach with flowers and clothes.

WOMAN.   These women have taken clothes from their dead
        to dress the boy's body.

During the following scene, HECUBA *gradually takes the clothes and wraps
the child.*

HECUBA.   I dress you for your burial
        with the same love I dressed you,
        living, for your play.
        My son's son, I love you more
        than I can say.

        Helen! You killed this boy.
        How shall you escape your punishment?
        If I could lay my hands on you now
        I'd rip your flesh to pieces
        shred by evil shred.
        Because of your whorish lust
        my son's son will break in dust.
        He's ready for the dead!

200

Your father's shield!
Lie under it! Lie still!
A part of me is glad to know
you never learned how to kill.

Men kill! They kill! They kill!
They never learn! They're stupid still!
I know war's stupid, they call it glory.
The lie endures, they call it history.

They strut and preen and swell with pride
and you are dead; and you are dead
and captive women will breed and die
while under your father' shield you lie.

FIRST WOMAN. The decent earth is waiting for the boy,
    decent and peaceful at the end of all,
    our most patient mother.

SECOND WOMAN. Peaceful and decent and calm and strong.

THIRD WOMAN. And witnessing the infinite wrong!

(HECUBA *has been performing funeral rites, symbolically staunching the* *wounds.*)

HECUBA. Broken thing, I'd make you whole again
    to live and play, to enjoy this mad world of men.
    I touch this wound, and this, and this;
    I still dream of your happiness.
    You're standing at a door in evening light,
    you are twenty years of age, the world is opening
    like a flower, a morning, an idea, a story
    and you are going to...
    Your burial rite!
    Let it be spoken!
    Leave me!
    Go to your father!
    (Bows her head, motionless, sees nothing.)

WOMAN. If I could,
    I'd take your grief on my own head.

HECUBA. Women, good women!
    Myself! My own!
    (She gets up, looks bewildered as if she'd had a vision.)

WOMAN. Yes, we are yours.
We are with you.

HECUBA. I stood before the face of God
and looked into his open hand.
His hand contained nothing,
only the black seeds of our destruction,
small black vital seeds in the hand of God.
I saw all our prayers
blown around his head
like dust in the wind.
If he reached out
he couldn't catch the dust.
The dust of all our prayers
will blow beyond
every known and unknown sea.
And then I saw us all,
us women who must bear
the murderous consequences of war,
I saw us all
gathered in God's hand.
And is he kind?
He turned us in his hand
he ruined what we cherished
crumbled our houses
shook our squares and streets
brought low our hopes
made our hills tremble
like children before bullies

until we knew that we had suffered
the most unspeakable wrong.

And then amid the dust, amid the wrong,
amid the trembling hills and cities
amid the streets of rubble and the fields of death

I heard the music of our hearts
I knew the everlasting beauty of the song
of earth and heaven.

I kissed God's hand! I am real. I am so real
I am not afraid to look into the eyes of God.

(*To the women.*) Bury him!

Clean his grave as best you can,
let him rot into reality!
We living have our dreams, our vanity.

The women take the body on the shield. Flames begin to rise from the city. Forms, shadows in the flames.

TALTHYBIUS. *(Comes out through the broken wall.)*
Burn everything in sight.
Burn everything until all this
is a huge, black, ashen circle
where a future man may stand and say
'There was a city here once!
People lived here! I don't believe it!'
Burn everything until there is no past.
Think of this city as an evil woman,
set fire to her flesh, her hair
rip our her heart, set fire to that,
stand back, enjoy the flames,
this is the best work you've ever done.

And ye – women – stand here
until you hear the trumpet call.
You'll hear it over every ruined wall
and when you do, go forward
to the ships.

And you, Hecuba; follow!
Odysseus has sent his men
to take you. Forget your dead!
Prepare your mind and body for a special bed!

HECUBA. You intend to destroy everything? Everything?

TALTHYBIUS. I am a go-between.
I know the two sides of this story.
I know that if anyone here, anyone,
man, woman, girl, boy,
has even the faintest seed of hope
in the farthest corner of his heart
all this work may go for nothing.
The work and purpose of my life is to destroy
everything that you hold dear,
every final seed of hope
you carry in your heart.

There's nothing more dangerous to a winner
than one seed of hope in the heart of the loser.
That's why everything must be destroyed.
You know what I'm saying.
I must kill your hope, Hecuba,
I am killing all your hope.

HECUBA. Are you?
Is this the death of hope?
The meaning of my life?
My city! Fire! Flower!
My flower of hope on fire!

Let me stand here
And look at my city on fire.

My city! You are a woman
eaten by fire!

That fire! It should be eating me!

I will go into the fire!

She goes toward the fire. The soldiers grab her.

TALTHYBIUS. Back!
Hold her for Odysseus.
Hold her!

I have never seen a spirit
To equal hers.

Hold her! Odysseus wants her!
Odysseus will have her!

WOMAN. We are women; we are children too.
What will we do?
Who will help us now?

FIRST WOMAN. God sees all this.
He has no pity.
Heartless, above us all, he watches
The burning and the shaming
and the raping of our city.
Heartless! Heartless!

SECOND WOMAN. I was reared there.
I knew first love there.

I tasted loss there.
I had children there.

Fire! All fire!

THIRD WOMAN. Smoke from the city on fire
rises and scatters.
Smoke is the lives of our men,
our sons and our daughters.
Smoke rises and scatters, pointless and free,
drifting over the sea.

HECUBA *kneels or falls and beats the earth with her hands.*

HECUBA. Earth, you are the mother of my children.
Let them hear my crying.
Children! Your hearts are listening,
there in the darkness lying.
Listen! Listen to me!

WOMAN. Hecuba is praying to the earth
and to the dead!

HECUBA. Listen! I pray again
to every buried shred of flesh and bone,
to every heart. Come near! Come near!
Come into my heart.
Live there, my dead father, mother, husband, sons,
live there, O my dead, as only you can live,
haunt every corner of my blood,
pour through me like a river
through a dying land.

WOMAN. I am near you, Hecuba, near you.
I hear you pray to your dead.
I am near you.
Let me pray to my dead.
My husband, hear my cry.

HECUBA. The dead are not the past, the dead are the future.
They listen and watch, their eyes
like glittering jewels
in the dark streets of eternity!

Listen, you dead!
I am a slave, Hecuba is a slave,
I must go to Odysseus, sleep with him.

205

I'd rather sleep with a giant rat.

Listen to that!

O my husband, listen to that!
Safe in your nothingness,
homeless and womanless,
know what I feel,
know what I am
in the hands of this man.

Look on my shame!
Do you know what it means
to suffer this?

Do you know? Answer, my husband!

Do you know? Answer, my husband!
Do you know what it means
to have this arrogant trickster, Odysseus,
play tricks with my body,
prowl through every secret of my body
like a smug conqueror exploring
the streets and laneways of a beautiful city?
Do you know what it means for me
to be abandoned by the man I loved,
to have his sympathy replaced by brute silence?
Speak to me! Answer me!
You have no right to silence!
An arrogant, tricky rat of a man claims me
and you are silent!
(HECUBA *beats the earth with her hands.*)

Damn you! Damn your silence! Damn your safe grave!
A man sends his messenger to me
to tell me I am his prize,
and I must go to him.
That man does not know or care who I am.
Who am I? I am a woman,
I am Hecuba, Hecuba, nobody but Hecuba,
I am not a prize, I am not a slave, not a slave
to anyone living or dead,
I am not a decoration or an ornament,
I am not a bit of scandal or a piece of gossip,
I am not something to be shown off or pointed at,

I am not something to be used at someone's beck and call,
I am not a thing, I am not a fuck,
I am telling you who I am,
I am telling you about the man
who is violating every last shred of my dignity,
whose every word is an insult to me
who wants me for his slave
who will have me in his bed.

(She beats the earth in rage, trying to make an impossible link.)

Answer me!
Answer me! You safe, cowardly, silent, blind, buried
bastard of a husband!
Let me hear your voice
through the earth and the grass and the stones.
Tell me what you think
of this insult I suffer
in the depths of my blood,
in the marrow of my bones.
Do you know what I suffer?
This insult? Do you know?

WOMAN. How can he know?
What can he say?

HECUBA. Let me tell you what has happened.
They have murdered the boy Astynax.
They've set fire to the city.
They have destroyed
everything you lived for, worked for, died for.

WOMAN. The living must forget the dead.
If there were no forgetfulness
who would dare to continue?
Then fire attacks our thought
when we remember that we forgot.
Let the dead rest in peace.
In peace let the dead rot.

HECUBA. Dust and smoke! Smoke and dust!
Nothing, nothing, but yes, yes,
final evidence of Helen's lust.
No curse known
to living or dead

is horrible enough
to fall on Helen's head.

Somewhere, there's a song for her.
A man will write it!
It will celebrate her beauty
and millions unborn will sing it.
The man who makes the song
will be so blinded by the blood of war,
he'll see nothing in the darkness of his mind
but Helen's beauty.
She is the mother of horror,
the origin of all our evil,
but the song will make her beautiful,
so beautiful
the horror will be forgotten,
forgotten by all except me
and women like me
who've seen the evil in her eyes,
her lips, her hands, her voice.
Beware the song of Helen's beauty!
I am not fooled by songs or plays
or tales or legends
because I have stood there, in the presence of men,
and seen Helen put her eyes to work
as if her eyes were the agents of her will;
I've seen her subtle hands make history
as other women make bread;
I've seen one eloquent movement of her head
turn critical men into worshippers;
I've seen the very air seduced
by magical ripples
of her sweet manipulating voice.
Her voice is her best song,
song of beauty, song of hell!

WOMAN. The smoke has a voice too,
a fat, black, thick, sluggish voice
that will make the sky sick.
What is the smokevoice saying?

A great crash is heard, the wall is lost in darkness.

WOMAN. Gone! All gone!

HECUBA. All around us, there are men.
Men fought the war,
destroyed the city,
chose us, set us apart,
decided we are prizes,
arranged our destinies.
Men wasted the land.
Men wait on the sea.
Men wait in the land beyond the sea.
And we must go into our future
as into a dark room.
Alone in that darkness,
out of mind, out of sight,
we will think, when we can,
of what was once
our City of Light, City of Peace.

WOMAN. Peace? What is peace?

HECUBA. Although men say they fight for peace,
peace is what they're most afraid of.
I remember a city, a street, a house.
I lived in peace there,
peace lived in me.
I loved in peace,
gave birth in peace,
reared my children in peace.
Then she came
and peace began to die.
As peace died
thousands of young men died with it.
Strange! Peace and youth must always
die together!
Peace died in women too
and yet you ask me, what is peace?
Peace is the shell of a burnt house,
peace is a child's body broken in the earth,
peace is a letter you have read a hundred times,
a cup or plate or chair or bed
buried under smoke and dust.

Smoke and dust! Dust and smoke!

(The trumpet sounds.)

Goodbye, goodbye, my city.
Burnt! Lost! Gone!
But still be in me,
be in my blood and in my dreams.

THE WOMEN. Goodbye, goodbye, our city.
Burnt! Lost! Gone!
But still be in us,
be in our blood and in our dreams.

The trumpet sounds again, the women vanish into the dark.

HECUBA. (*Remains standing when the others have gone.*)
There's a man at your side,
there's a man in your mind,
there's a man in your bed:
these men are strangers you've decided to grow used to
because you know them too much, too much.
What are we to make of the strangers
we are to each other and to ourselves?
What does it matter if I sleep with a stranger
here or in another country?
What does it matter if I must
swallow the sour, foul seed
of his vain and suffocating lust?
What does it matter if I fuck
some tricky itchy stinking weasel of a Greek
so long as I know what I'm doing
and why I'm doing it?
And when he's fucking me
may I not smile
and ask the very face of darkness –
darling, who is free?

What does he see? What does he think he sees?
What does he know of me
when he shrinks back into himself, alone,
like a snail shrivelling at my touch,
a man shrivelled with fulfilment,
puny with success, a worm limp with victory,
alone?
Alone,
may I not open or close my eyes,
relishing the part of me that he can never reach,

that no man living can ever reach?
I have a power no man can ever touch.
Although a man may fall asleep at my side,
snoring in fulfilment, fat with vanity,
he'll never dream there is a sea between us.
I can explore that sea
until I find the stranger living in myself
and get to know her and her cold power
as I have never known a man
or permitted any man to know me.
I can walk, talk, think, cry, surprise myself,
I can wonder who I am
and not break apart in madness
because I don't have an answer.
I can look at the rage and hatred in my heart
and know them for what they are –
hatred and rage. Mine!
And I can taste them
as I have tasted love.
I can smell a man
in me, outside me.
I can smell him on my skin,
in the air about me,
and know the kind of stranger that he is.

The darkness deepens. Deep as the sea.
My mind is clear.
What's before me?
The sea! The sea!
Let whatever must happen, happen to me.
I am Hecuba, I am
what life and death have forced me to be.
I know love is a wound and its blood is life.
I have tried to make a space for love.
I have to leave this place. How?
I have to go somewhere. Where?
How shall I go?
I shall put one leg in front of the other
and shuffle towards tonight and tomorrow,
towards a man and his plans,
a man and his fantasy.
One leg in front of the other. So.
That is how I shall reach the sea

and know it for what it is
stretching before me
like all the questions of my life
growing out of each other,
chasing each other
like waves, waves that cannot rest,
like me,
Hecuba, a wave of the sea.

A wave of the sea!
Natural and fearless!
That is what I want –
I want to live without fear
and I will, I will,
no matter where I happen to be,
Hecuba, a woman, Hecuba,
a natural, fearless wave of the sea.

Waves waves waves waves waves
endless unknown driven
dreams in the hearts of women.
Nobody can count the waves,
nobody can count the waves,
the waves tell more
than the waves themselves can ever be,
the waves outnumber every thought
possible to you and me.
The waves roar and moan in pain.
The waves laugh happily.
The waves are slaves.
The waves are free.
The war is over. The war begins – for me!

She goes out slowly.